INTRODUCTION TO
THE ROMANS

INTRODUCTION TO
THE ROMANS

CHARTWELL
BOOKS, INC.

LESLEY AND ROY ADKINS

This book is dedicated to Jim and Mavis Lock

A QUINTET BOOK

Published by Chartwell Books
A Division of Book Sales, Inc.
110 Enterprise Avenue
Secaucus, New Jersey 07094

This edition is produced for sale in North
America, its territories and dependencies only.

ISBN 1-55521-709-5

This book was designed and produced by
Quintet Publishing Limited
6, Blundell Street
London N7 9BH

Creative Director: Terry Jeavons
Designer: Stuart Walden
Project Editor: Caroline Beattie
Editor: Sarah Buckley
Illustration: Danny McBride

Typeset in Great Britain by
Central Southern Typesetters, Eastbourne
Manufactured in Hong Kong by
Regent Publishing Services Limited
Printed in Hong Kong by
Leefung-Asco Printers Limited

CONTENTS

INTRODUCTION

The Roman Empire died out nearly 1,500 years ago but, unlike other civilizations in the world which have been long forgotten, the legacy of the Romans is still with us today. The very word 'Romans' covered many races across a vast empire, and did not just refer to people living in Rome. In this book we have given an account of the history and a description of life in the Roman world from its beginnings in 753 BC to the emergence of the Byzantine Empire in the east, over 1,000 years later.

Chapter 1 describes the founding of Rome, the seven kings of Rome, and the development of the Republic and its early history. Chapter 2 describes the end of the Republic and the beginning of the Empire after the power struggles of Pompey the Great, Julius Caesar, Antony and finally Octavian who became the Emperor Augustus in 27 BC. The development of the early years of the Empire is outlined, including the conquest of land from Scotland to Syria. Later on, the Empire was split into two parts, East and West, and Constantine I chose what is now Istanbul as his capital city.

For those interested in military affairs, Chapter 3 describes the Roman army, its weapons, armour, forts and frontiers. This is followed by six chapters on aspects of the social and everyday life of the Roman world, including towns, water supply, countryside villas, slavery, entertainment, crafts and industries, roads and transport, ships, gods and temples. The final chapter takes up the history of the Roman Empire from the time of Constantine I to the collapse of the Western Empire and its reconquest by the Byzantine Empire. Finally, we look at how evidence of Roman civilization, from small statues to whole towns, has survived to the present day (although now rapidly being destroyed by modern development), and how the legacy of the Romans influences everyone's lives.

RIGHT A shop in Ostia near Rome which prepared and sold food.

OPPOSITE The impressive Pont du Gard was part of the aqueduct serving Nîmes in southern Gaul, at the point where it crossed the River Gard. It was built on a series of arches, and the lower part was widened in the 18th century to take road traffic.

CHAPTER ONE

The
RISE
of
ROME

"Rome was not built in a day."
(ANONYMOUS, MEDIEVAL PROVERB)

THE FOUNDATION OF ROME

Rome was not built in a day, nor did it fall overnight. Rome rose from a small village to become a powerful, wealthy city-state controlling a vast empire. Although the empire collapsed, its legacy survives today, one and a half thousand years later.

According to ancient tradition, Rome was founded in 753 BC, but its origins were much disputed even by Roman historians. As there were no early written records documenting Rome's origins, the history of this time is a mixture of legend, mythology and fact. In the 5th century BC, Greek historians wrote that Rome was founded by the Trojan hero Aeneas. He was a mythological figure (the son of Venus by Anchises) who was supposed to have fled to Italy after the sack of Troy (which occurred in the 12th century BC).

Another explanation was that the twins Romulus and Remus were abandoned as children on the banks of the River Tiber. They were saved and suckled by a she-wolf, and then rescued by a shepherd who brought them up on the left bank of the river. It was there, on the Palatine Hill, that Romulus later founded the city of Rome, having killed his brother Remus in a quarrel.

As there were insufficient women in Rome, Romulus arranged for women to be abducted from the nearby Sabine tribe (an incident often referred to as "the rape of the Sabine women"). He also chose one hundred 'fathers'

ABOVE *According to legend, the twins Romulus and Remus were abandoned as children on the banks of the River Tiber. They were saved and suckled by a she-wolf, and in 753 BC Romulus founded the city of Rome.*

(*patres*) to advise him, a group which developed into the first Senate or ruling council. The descendants of these men were known as patricians and represented the leading families of Rome. Gradually, the legends became conflated and Romulus came to be regarded as a direct descendant of Aeneas.

Early on in Rome's history, the Greeks were establishing colonies in southern Italy to facilitate trade in the area. There were also many other different peoples and tribes throughout Italy, with numerous languages and dialects being spoken. The inhabitants of Rome mainly spoke Latin and, as Rome eventually gained control of Italy, the use of Latin became widespread.

LEFT *The city of Rome developed from a cluster of small villages. The forum is situated on former marshland which was drained in the time of Tarquin I.*

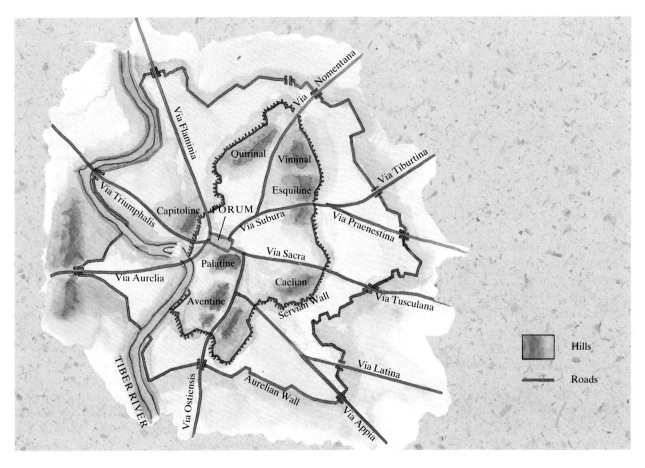

ABOVE The city of Rome in the imperial period with the seven hills which it first occupied.

The city of Rome occupied the seven hills and the intervening valleys near the mouth of the River Tiber, in the territory known then as Latium. Archaeological evidence from this area suggests that from the 10th century BC (in the latter part of the Bronze Age), there was small-scale occupation in villages of wooden huts perched on the hilltops, with cemeteries in the marshy valleys below. From about 900 BC (in the Iron Age), these village settlements expanded and their cemeteries had some rich graves which indicate a developing social structure to match. By the late 7th century BC there were some extremely rich grave goods left behind.

From around 640 BC, many towns were established by different tribes in Latium but Rome became pre-eminent. By the late 7th century BC, Rome's various hilltop villages had merged into a single settlement and occupation had spread into the marshy valleys which were by then being drained. By the beginning of the 6th century BC, Rome had become an urbanized settlement, possessing masonry structures such as temples, sanctuaries and defensive walls. There was also a public square laid out on former marshland

in an area which was later to become the Forum. All this building work has been credited to the initiative of Tarquin I who ruled from 616 to 579 BC.

THE SEVEN KINGS

Including the legendary figure Romulus, there were seven kings of Rome. Much of the history of the kings was related by the Roman historian Livy (59 BC – AD 17), writing some 600 years after these events took place, and is therefore a mixture of fact and folklore. The kings were not hereditary but were chosen by the Senate. Initially, they were of Latin or Sabine extraction, until 616 BC when Tarquin I became the first of three Etruscan kings. The Etruscan tribe had controlled much of central and northern Italy from the 8th century BC, and had established many cities. Although Rome accepted the Etruscans as kings, the city did not come under Etruscan domination; nevertheless, it was greatly influenced by Etruscan civilization, particularly in architecture and art. From the time of Tarquin I, the appearance of Rome was transformed by a great deal of building work initiated by him.

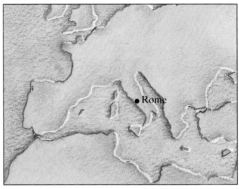

THE EARLY REPUBLIC

In 509 BC, when the tyrannical king Tarquin the Proud was expelled due to his immense unpopularity, the monarchy ended and the Republic was born. The kings were replaced by two magistrates, initially called praetors and later consuls, elected annually from members of the Senate. In addition, there were various other hierarchical categories of leadership which underwent constant modification throughout the Republic. One major innovation occurred in 494 BC, when the plebeians (the urban poor) reacted against their oppression and debt, and established a system of officers called tribunes to act on their behalf.

Rome at first dominated the surrounding Latin cities, and in 509 BC there was a treaty between Rome and Carthage (now in Tunisia) affording protection to these cities. Carthage was the main city of the Phoenicians (originally from what is now the Lebanon). They had settled in this part of North Africa and became a powerful seafaring nation. The Latin tribes subsequently entered into conflict with Rome and a lengthy military struggle began which Rome won in 499 BC. A treaty was signed leading to the establishment of the Latin League, and a joint army was created. Further hostilities with other tribes in Italy continued to erupt throughout the 5th century BC, including war with the Etruscan city of Veii situated about 9 miles (15km) north of Rome. During this war Veii was besieged for 10 years until 396 BC, when it was captured and destroyed. Rome's territory was consequently greatly increased.

THE INVASION OF THE GAULS

During the 5th century BC, the Gauls (Celtic peoples who inhabited Gaul, now modern-

ROME'S EARLIEST RULERS	
753 BC	Foundation of Rome
753–715 BC	Romulus
715–673 BC	Numa Pompilius (Sabine)
673–641 BC	Tullus Hostilius (Latin)
641–616 BC	Ancus Marcius (Sabine)
616–579 BC	L. Tarquinius Priscus, Tarquin I (Etruscan)
579–534 BC	Servius Tullius (Etruscan)
534–509 BC	L. Tarquinius Superbus, Tarquin II or Tarquin the Proud (Etruscan)
509 BC	Foundation of the Republic

ABOVE At times of crisis throughout Roman history, strong men appeared to take charge of the destiny of the state. Caracalla became sole emperor from 211–217 AD after he murdered his brother Geta (see p.31).

TOP RIGHT Rome occupied a central, strategic position in the Italian peninsula. Surrounded by hostile tribes, it was early Roman policy to either conquer them or win them over as allies.

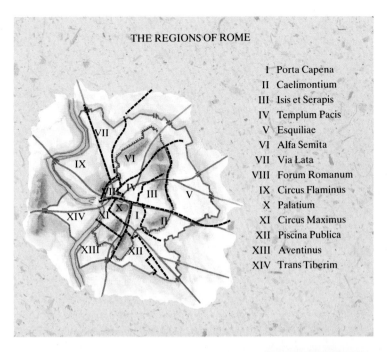

THE REGIONS OF ROME

I	Porta Capena
II	Caelimontium
III	Isis et Serapis
IV	Templum Pacis
V	Esquiliae
VI	Alfa Semita
VII	Via Lata
VIII	Forum Romanum
IX	Circus Flaminus
X	Palatium
XI	Circus Maximus
XII	Piscina Publica
XIII	Aventinus
XIV	Trans Tiberim

ABOVE TOP Augustus divided the city of Rome into four administrative districts. The earlier and later walls around Rome are shown here as well.

ABOVE A model of Rome in the imperial period, with the River Tiber below, the Colosseum top left, and the Circus Maximus in the centre.

day France and part of Germany) were pushing across the Alps into Italy in search of new homelands, and in 391 BC a force of 30,000 Gauls crossed the Apennines. In July of the following year the Roman army, which attempted to stop the invasions, was routed and the Gauls entered Rome with no resistance. The city was sacked but the Capitol (the citadel and religious centre) held out for seven months. Although the Gauls then left Rome with their plundered goods, it took another two centuries for them to be totally removed from northern Italy. There is in fact very little archaeological evidence for this disaster, suggesting that it may have been exaggerated by the Roman historians who later recorded the incident.

The rebuilding of Rome began almost immediately after the sacking of the city. From 378 BC a massive new defensive wall – the Servian Wall – was constructed, and it apparently partly followed the line of an earlier city wall constructed by King Servius Tullius in the 6th century BC.

THE CONQUEST OF ITALY

After the setback of the Gaulish invasion, Rome again became increasingly involved in its neighbours' affairs by assisting some tribes in fighting against others. Throughout the next century there was a series of conflicts with opponents in Italy, in particular with the Samnite tribe to the south who were eventually forced to become allies of Rome in 290 BC. From controlling a small area around the city, Rome came to dominate much of Italy in its bid for power, wealth and stability.

In the late 4th and early 3rd centuries BC, the Romans became much influenced by Greek culture, including architecture, religion and the arts. It was about this time that the Roman state first issued silver coins which were modelled on the coinage of the south Italian Greek cities. By the beginning of the 3rd century BC, the Greek cities in southern Italy were in decline, and Rome came to the assistance of some of those being harassed by the nearby Lucanian tribe. The Greek city of Tarentum (now Tarento) regarded this as a threat to its own independence and appealed to King Pyrrhus of Epirus for assistance. Pyrrhus intially achieved a number of victories over the Romans, but sustained heavy losses (hence the term 'Pyrrhic victory') and in 275 BC he was eventually defeated. For the Greeks to be defeated by the Romans was unprecedented, and Rome consequently pressed home this victory and took control of the southern Italian peninsula.

Rome's conquest of Italy involved incorporating its defeated enemies as Roman citizens or half-citizens, or compelling them to become allies. Large areas of territory were annexed and colonies founded which were settled mainly by the urban poor. The system of alliances and dependencies created by the Romans during the conquest of the Italian peninsula became known as the Roman Confederacy.

By 260 BC the tribes of central and southern Italy had lost their independence. The cultural and linguistic differences in the Italian peninsula gradually disappeared and Latin became the common language. A network of military roads linking the Latin colonies accelerated this process of Romanization.

THE PUNIC WARS

The First Punic War began in 264 BC, so-called because it was fought against the Phoenicians (Carthaginians) who were called 'Poeni' by the Romans, from which the English term 'Punic' is derived. This marked the first conflict overseas and, until then, Rome had possessed little naval power because the seas of the western Mediterranean were controlled by Greece and by Carthage. Rome had previously entered into treaties with Carthage but, following a minor incident in Sicily, subsequently waged a lengthy and costly conflict with the Carthaginians. In order to fight them effectively, Rome was forced to increase vastly the size of its own naval fleet. Even so, the war dragged on for 23 years until 241 BC when the Romans finally won a decisive naval victory off the western coast of Sicily, the battle of the 'Aegates Islands'. The Carthaginians agreed to give up all claim to Sicily and thereafter Rome gained control of Sardinia and Corsica as well. Both sides suffered huge losses in the war, and it is calculated that the Romans alone lost over 100,000 men and 500 warships.

The Second Punic War began only four years later when Carthage attempted to reassert itself by securing land in Spain. The Romans did not come into direct conflict with Carthage until 219 BC when General Hannibal continued to enlarge Carthaginian territory by attacking the town of Saguntum (now Sagunto), an ally of Rome on the Mediterranean coast. Before Rome could take retaliatory action, Hannibal marched out of Spain and made his famous trek across the Alps with elephants and a huge force of infantry and cavalry. He marched into Italy in 218 BC, and over the next two years inflicted a series of defeats on the Roman army, culminating in the battle of Cannae when at least 30,000 Romans lost their lives.

Despite these victories by Hannibal, most of Rome's allies tended to remain loyal, and Hannibal was eventually forced to leave Italy. In 203 BC he returned to North Africa but was defeated by the Romans at Zama (now in Tunisia) and was driven into exile and subsequently to suicide. As punishment, Carthage

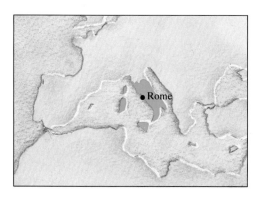

RIGHT By the 3rd century BC Rome's territory covered much of Italy.

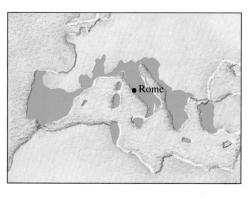

RIGHT After the First Punic War, Rome was in control of Sardinia, Corsica, Sicily and much of the Italian peninsula.

RIGHT Rome's territory had expanded considerably by the late 2nd century BC and extended from Portugal to Asia Minor.

was made to pay a massive indemnity, to destroy its fleet, and to give up all overseas territory. Thus Rome gained control of what is now south-west and eastern Spain, which was then divided into two provinces, Hispania Ulterior and Hispania Citerior. The few towns and tribes in Italy which had supported Hannibal were also punished.

The Third Punic War broke out when Rome intervened in a dispute between Carthage and Rome's friend and ally, King Masinissa of Numidia (now part of Algeria and Tunisia, and whose Latin name was derived from the Greek *nomades* or nomads). The Roman Senate was persuaded to destroy Carthage and sent a force which, after besieging the city for two years, attacked it and razed it to the ground in 146 BC. The territory belonging to Carthage became the new

Roman province known as Africa (situated today in North Africa).

THE CAMPAIGNS IN NORTHERN ITALY

Meanwhile, by the late 3rd century BC, those Gauls who lived in northern Italy were becoming restless. They were particularly provoked by being evicted from their land which was then allotted to Roman citizens. In 225 BC a huge Gaulish army crossed the Apennines, but was defeated by the Romans at Telamon (now Talamone), and the Gauls were forced back across the mountains. The Roman army then advanced into the Po Valley and began to take over large parts of the borders of Italy and France (an area known to the Romans as Gallia Cisalpina, usually referred to as Cisalpine Gaul). In 218 BC a large colony was established at Placentia (Piacenza) and another at Cremona in northern Italy.

The process of integrating Cisalpine Gaul with Roman Italy was halted by Hannibal's invasion, but military action in this area was resumed in 203 BC. Most of the Gaulish tribes here were defeated over the next twenty years, and Roman colonies were set up.

GREECE AND MACEDONIA

Alexander the Great died in 323 BC and his vast empire was fragmented into competing states ruled by his generals. By 275 BC three main kingdoms had emerged – Egypt under Ptolemy; Greece and the Aegean under Antigonus Gonatas; Asia Minor, Syria and the east under Seleucus. A new Greek kingdom with its capital at Pergamum was subsequently formed out of Seleucid territory in western Turkey, and was ruled by the Attalids.

In 229–228 BC Rome attacked the pirates operating along the Illyrian coast (now Yugoslavia); this campaign is known as the First Illyrian War. Macedonia (now mainly northern Greece) supported the pirates and became an enemy of Rome when the pirates' stronghold was destroyed in a second campaign in 221–219 BC (the Second Illyrian War). From 202 BC Philip V, King of Macedonia, began to take control of other areas of Greece and so, two years later, a Roman force was sent against him. This successful campaign forced Philip to confine his activities to Macedonia. At this time, Rome preferred a policy of indirect rule in the Greek

east, leaving the territory as a network of theoretically independent 'client states', and so in 196 BC the Romans withdrew from Greece. In the same year, though, the Seleucid king of Asia Minor, Antiochus III, invaded Greece. A Roman force was sent back, and in 191 BC it won a victory at the famous pass of Thermopylae, driving Antiochus out of Greece. The Romans then invaded what is now Turkey and defeated Antiochus III at Magnesia in 190 BC.

In 171 BC Rome went to war against Macedonia, which was becoming an increasingly

powerful state. Perseus (son of Philip V who had died eight years earlier) was eventually defeated in 168 BC at the battle of Pydna where his army was virtually destroyed. Macedonia was then split into four self-governing territories but, after an uprising in 148 BC, Rome annexed Macedonia as a province. A further revolt which followed in the southern peninsula of Greece (Achaea) was also suppressed, and its territory was made part of the new province. As an example to the rest of the empire, the city of Corinth was destroyed and its citizens sold into slavery in

ABOVE Following Rome's victory in the Third Punic War, much of North Africa became a new province. It soon became an important agricultural state, supplying Rome with much-needed grain. This mosaic from Tunisia depicts a villa surrounded by fowl and trees.

146 BC, the same year in which Carthage was razed to the ground.

From the late 3rd century BC, the kingdom of Pergamum (now in western Turkey) had been an important ally of Rome. When Attalus III, the last king of Pergamum, died in 133 BC, he bequeathed his kingdom to Rome and five years later it became the province known as Asia. In less than 150 years from the beginning of the First Punic War, Rome's territory had expanded to incorporate parts of modern Northern Africa, Spain, Greece and Turkey.

LEFT Due to an uprising in southern Greece, the city of Corinth was destroyed in 146 BC as an example to the rest of the empire, and its citizens were sold into slavery. A Roman colony was founded on the site a century later.

CHAPTER TWO

CONQUEST
and
CONSOLIDATION

*"Render therefore unto Caesar
the things which are Caesar's."*
(ST MATTHEW'S GOSPEL, 22:21)

THE END OF THE REPUBLIC

By the late 2nd century BC, serious disturbances were occurring throughout Italy, due mainly to the worsening plight of the rural and urban poor. In 133 BC Tiberius Gracchus, who had been elected a tribune, initiated land reforms, including the re-settling of dispossessed peasants on allotments of land. Intense opposition was aroused in many quarters to his proposals, and when he announced his intention to stand for a second tribunate, he was killed in the subsequent riots, with many of his supporters. Further unrest followed, and his brother Gaius Gracchus was elected a tribune in 123 and 122 BC. He introduced wide-ranging economic and legislative reforms but gradually lost popularity. In 121 BC he was declared a public enemy by the Senate and, soon after, he and 3,000 of his supporters were put to death.

Towards the end of the 2nd century BC, the military generals rose to power and this resulted in decades of civil strife. After the destruction of Corinth and Carthage in 146 BC there was a collapse in the stability of the Roman political way of life, with hostility

ABOVE The end of the 2nd century BC was a bleak period in Rome's fortunes, and in 105 BC a Roman army was annihilated at Arausio (now Orange) in southern Gaul, where this arch was constructed over a century later when Rome was again in the ascendant.

and turmoil in all parts of the Empire. Furthermore, Rome began to suffer a series of humiliating military defeats – in 105 BC an army was annihilated at Arausio (now Orange in France) by Germanic tribes advancing towards Italy. At that moment, the State of Rome was faced with extinction.

Gaius Marius (155–86 BC) had been elected consul in 108 BC and his first major task was to lead the war against the Numidians in North Africa, whom he defeated in 105 BC, the same year as the disaster at Arausio. To achieve military success Marius completely reformed the army, whose soldiers then began to owe allegiance to their commanders rather than to the State. This allowed the military commanders to use the armies for their own political ambitions, and eventually led to various civil wars. After the North African campaign, Marius was appointed to save Italy from the Germanic tribes, and his forces defeated the Teutones at Aquae Sextiae (now Aix-en-Provence) in 102 BC and the Cimbri at Vercellae (now Vercelli) the following year.

There was increasing unrest amongst the inhabitants of Italy, resentful at being exploited by Rome. As a result, an armed revolt broke out in 91 BC which is known as the Social War (from *socii*, allies). Within two years the war was largely over, Roman citizenship having been granted to many of Italy's inhabitants in 90 BC. This gave them greater participation in politics, including an opportunity to enter the Senate.

In 88 BC Lucius Cornelius Sulla (137–78 BC) was elected consul. He was asked to lead an army in the eastern Mediterranean to suppress Mithridates VI, King of Pontus (an area around the Black Sea), who had been provoked into invading the province of Asia, had massacred Roman citizens, and afterwards invaded Greece and the Aegean islands. Sulla's appointment led to much bitter conflict between him and Marius and their supporters. For three years from 87 BC Sulla campaigned in the east and, although Marius died in 86 BC, civil war still broke out between their supporters three years later. On his return from the east, Sulla was forced to march on Rome to oppose the supporters of Marius, where he carried out a purge of his opponents in which thousands are supposed to have died. Sulla had himself been appointed dictator in 81 BC, and passed a series of laws; he retired the following year and died in 78 BC.

THE FIRST TRIUMVIRATE

One of the generals to emerge during Sulla's period of power was Gnaeus Pompeius (later called Magnus, or Pompey the Great). He was the most powerful general of the 70s and 60s BC, and, in his own lifetime, was compared with Alexander the Great. He achieved particular military success in Spain in the 70s, and in 71 BC helped Crassus to put down the slave revolt of Spartacus in Italy. Pompey stood for the office of consul with Crassus in the following year, although he was not legally qualified to do so. Three years later he managed to clear the seas around Italy of the pirates who had been preying on shipping and coastal settlements. In the east, Mithridates was again active and Pompey took control of campaigns there for four years, conquering Anatolia (part of Turkey) and Syria, thereby acquiring much new territory for Rome. He advanced as far as Jerusalem, and returned to Rome in 62 BC with enormous quantities of booty.

During Pompey's absence in the east, Crassus and Caesar built up their own politi-

JULIUS CAESAR

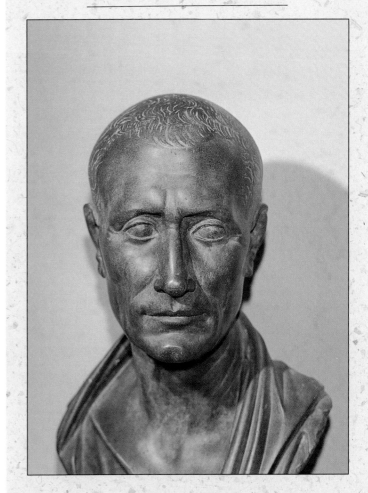

ABOVE Julius Caesar became dictator after the defeat of Pompey the Great in 48 BC. Four years later he was assassinated on the Ides of March, and has been immortalized in William Shakespeare's play Julius Caesar.

cal positions. They proposed a bill to give land to the poor and to Pompey's veterans, but this was opposed by the Senate. Together with Pompey, Crassus and Caesar formed a private alliance in 60 BC, known as the First Triumvirate; this was a power base enabling their political wishes to be fulfilled. Marcus Licinius Crassus (115–53 BC) was a wealthy, unscrupulous politician who had been consul with Pompey in 70 BC. He went to Syria in 54 BC, but was killed the following year in a disastrous defeat by the Parthians (a tribe who occupied modern-day Iran) at the battle of Carrhae (now Harran in eastern Turkey).

Gaius Julius Caesar (100–44 BC) belonged

RIGHT Legionary soldiers being addressed by their Emperor. Standard-bearers wearing animal skins are holding the standards. The soldiers are wearing either segmented plate armour or overlapping scale armour and are holding javelins.

CONQUEST OF EGYPT

ABOVE The defeat of Antony and Cleopatra by Octavian led to Egypt becoming a Roman province. People from this area were settled at Nemausus (Nîmes) in southern Gaul, and this was celebrated at the time by coins featuring a crocodile chained to a palm tree. This is still used as a civic symbol at Nîmes today, as shown on this brass plaque.

to a patrician family which allegedly traced its roots back to Aeneas. After the dictatorship of Sulla, Caesar had sought popularity by associating himself with Pompey and Crassus. With their support, he became consul for 59 BC and, as he needed military success, he persuaded the Senate to give him command of Cisalpine Gaul and also Gallia Narbonensis (an area of southern France) for five years. He then achieved considerable military success in Gaul and Britain.

In 56 BC the triumvirate alliance was renewed, but two years later Pompey's wife Julia (Caesar's daughter) died. This caused the already weakened alliance to split further, and it ceased to exist when Crassus died. Meanwhile, in Rome, there was civil disorder but Pompey, who was made sole consul in 52 BC, restored order. Fear of Caesar's in-

creasing power through his military successes led the Senate, in 49 BC, to vote that he should relinquish his command, and so on 11 January of that year Caesar invaded Italy, beginning a civil war. Pompey did not confront Caesar but withdrew to the east, to be defeated by Caesar the following year at Pharsalus (now Pharsala) in Greece. After escaping to Egypt, Pompey was murdered, and Caesar suppressed all other opposition. He became dictator, but four years later in 44 BC was assassinated on the Ides of March (15 March), which led to renewed civil war.

THE SECOND TRIUMVIRATE

When Caesar was assassinated, the official Heads of State were Marcus Antonius (Mark Antony) and Marcus Aemilius Lepidus. However, in his will Caesar had nominated his great-nephew Octavian as his heir, who then assumed the name of Caesar as a way of advancing his career. Octavian (Gaius Julius Caesar Octavianus) returned to Rome on Caesar's death to be welcomed by supporters of Caesar. When Antony went to Cisalpine Gaul in 43 BC, the Senate was persuaded that his aim was to become dictator. Octavian was therefore sent against him together with the two consuls, and Antony was defeated in two battles near Mutina (now Modena) in northern Italy, but the two consuls were killed. Octavian then demanded the office of consul, which the Senate refused, and so he marched on Rome with his army and took it by force. Meanwhile, Lepidus, who had control of seven legions in Gallia Narbonensis, joined forces with Antony. Octavian decided to meet Antony and Lepidus, and they were reconciled, forming the Second Triumvirate in 43 BC, this time a legal dictatorship which was created for five years.

The following year, Lepidus served as consul while Antony and Octavian went to war in the east against their opponents Brutus and Cassius. Numerous political murders followed. In 40 BC Lepidus was given charge of Africa, Octavian the West, and Antony the East. Lepidus made an unsuccessful bid for power four years later and, although his life was spared, his political career was finished.

During his campaigns in the east, Antony suffered several disasters in Armenia in 36 BC. He also became increasingly involved with Cleopatra, Queen of Egypt, and Octavian used this as propaganda against him. The Triumvirate was not renewed when it expired and, two years later in 31 BC when Antony was deprived of his powers by the Senate, Octavian obtained a mandate to go to war against Cleopatra. He followed Antony and Cleopatra to Greece, defeating Antony in a naval battle off Actium. Antony fled with Cleopatra to Egypt but, pursued by Octavian, they committed suicide there in 30 BC.

Octavian claimed to have restored the Republic in 27 BC, but in reality he was left in sole charge of the Roman world which by then had grown into an empire. Up until the battle of Actium, Rome had been close to anarchy, but in a few years Octavian restored stability and undertook fundamental reforms which were to remain more or less intact for 300 years. He gave land to thousands of soldiers and removed the army from the political scene. In 19 BC Augustus (the name he had assumed) was granted consular power for life. He died 32 years later, aged 77, in AD 14.

THE EMPERORS

Augustus ruled as emperor from 27 BC to AD 14, and one aspect of his 41-year reign was the vast programme of public building that he initiated. According to the Roman writer Suetonius, Augustus claimed to have found Rome a city of bricks but left it a city of marble. Since Augustus' first two choices of successor died during his lifetime, he forced Tiberius, his stepson from his third marriage to Livia, to divorce his wife Vipsania Agrippina in 12 BC and marry Augustus' daughter Julia instead.

On Augustus' death Tiberius was accepted as his successor by the Senate, thereby setting the precedent of dynastic inheritance. Up to the mid-3rd century, there was a series of stable dynasties punctuated by occasional civil wars, but in the 3rd century there was a

BELOW A sardonyx cameo portraying Augustus. He became the first emperor of the Roman world after a period of civil war which ended in the defeat of Antony and Cleopatra. The gold chain was added to the cameo in the Middle Ages.

Left Augustus originally wanted his grandsons Gaius and Lucius Caesar to be his successors, but they died prematurely. This mausoleum to commemorate them was built at Glanum, in southern Gaul.

rapid succession of emperors, and it was only after the rise of Constantine I, the Great, in the early 4th century that stability with dynastic succession was restored. Much is known of the lives of the emperors through Roman and Greek historians, but a great deal of their writing is coloured by bias and exaggeration, leading to misconceptions and uncertainties about the various reigns.

Tiberius' reign was relatively well-run and stable in its earlier years, but it became notorious for its period of terror. Tiberius spent the last ten years of his life in voluntary seclusion on the island of Capri, and his death in 37 was greeted with joy. His successor was his great-nephew Gaius, nicknamed Caligula – Little Boots – because of the little soldier's boots he wore as a child. He led an unbalanced reign, believing himself to be a god, and was assassinated after only four years as emperor. Tiberius Claudius Nero Germanicus (usually called Claudius) suc-

ceeded Caligula in 41, and is best known for the invasion of Britain that he undertook two years later. There are widely varying opinions about his reign, some considering him to have been weak-willed, ruled by his advisers and family, and others that he reigned with

RIGHT Claudius (41–54) became emperor after Caligula was assassinated, and he was responsible for the invasion of Britain in 43. He is particularly well-known because of Robert Graves' book I, Claudius.

LEFT A 19th-century portrayal of the invasion of Britain in 43 under the Emperor Claudius. The Roman army has landed on the seashore, and the legionary standard-bearer calls on his colleagues to follow. The exact point of landing is much disputed by historians.

particular adroitness. Claudius died in 54, allegedly having eaten poisoned mushrooms administered by his wife Agrippina in order to promote her son Nero as emperor.

Nero's reign degenerated into cruelty and tyranny, and he may even have been responsible for his mother's murder. While he was emperor there was a serious rebellion in Britain led by Queen Boudicca who was eventually defeated, and a more prolonged and serious rebellion in Judaea, eventually put down by Titus. When a great fire at Rome in 64 was blamed on Nero (because it was thought that he wanted to build himself a vast new capital in the ruins), he tried to hold the Christians responsible, and increased his persecution of this unpopular new sect. The fire was so devastating that only four out of Rome's fourteen districts survived intact, leading to a massive rebuilding programme by Nero, including the 'Golden House', a huge urban villa for himself, the construction of which caused much resentment.

In the spring of 68, a Gallic senator Julius Vindex, then a governor in Gaul, stirred up a revolt against Nero, and persuaded the elderly governor of Spain, Servicius Sulpicius Galba, to be proclaimed emperor. This drove Nero to commit suicide in June 68 at the age of 32. A few months later in 69, Aulus Vitellius, who had been sent by Galba to take command of Lower Germany, was proclaimed emperor by his troops stationed there. Soon afterwards, Otho was proclaimed emperor by the Praetorian Guard at Rome, and Galba was murdered, but Vitellius, with his forces, marched against Otho, who committed suicide in April 69. In the east, the armies of Flavius Vespasianus (Vespasian) proclaimed him emperor. Vespasian defeated and killed Vitellius and became emperor, thus ending the chaotic 'year of the four emperors' and founding the Flavian dynasty. His 10-year rule marked a new period of stability in the Roman Empire.

Vespasian's son Titus succeeded in 79, the same year in which the volcano Vesuvius erupted and destroyed the towns of Pompeii and Herculanium in southern Italy. A few years earlier, Titus had undertaken ruthless military campaigns against the Jews in Judaea, and in 70 he captured Jerusalem and destroyed its temple. As an emperor, Titus was popular, but died through ill-health after only two years' reign at the age of 41, and his

LEFT Nero (54–68) committed suicide at the age of 32 after a reign which degenerated into cruelty and tyranny. While he was emperor, there was a devastating fire at Rome which was blamed on him.

Left Trajan's Column in Rome has a spiral frieze depicting the campaign against Dacia. Here soldiers are constructing a camp from blocks of turf. The Empire reached its greatest extent under the Emperor Trajan.

younger brother Domitian became emperor.

During Domitian's reign, the administration of most of the provinces functioned well, but towards the end of his lifetime he became increasingly autocratic and tended to ignore the role of the Senate. He was particularly notorious for his serious persecutions of the Christians and Jews. He was murdered in 96, apparently in a plot involving his wife. The elderly and respected senator Nerva was chosen as emperor by the Senate. As he had no son, Nerva appointed Marcus Ulpius Trajanus (Trajan) as his successor and established the tradition of appointment by merit. Shortly afterwards, in 98, Nerva died and

Trajan assumed the leadership, reigning until his own death 19 years later. Under Trajan, the Empire expanded to its greatest extent, from Scotland to Africa, and from Portugal to Syria. His most important campaign was against Dacia (an area to the north of the River Danube roughly equivalent to modern-day Romania). His triumph was celebrated on a spiral frieze on the commemorative column still standing in Rome and known as Trajan's Column.

Hadrian, also from Spain (from a town called Italica, north of Seville), had been adopted as Trajan's successor and assumed power in 117. To consolidate Trajan's con-

quests he abandoned some of the latter's annexations. During his 21-year reign, Hadrian travelled extensively around the Empire, and during a visit to Britain in 122 he authorized the construction of what is now known as Hadrian's Wall across northern England. In 138 Antoninus Pius became emperor, and in the latter years of his life ruled jointly with Marcus Aurelius, his adopted son. On Pius' death in 161, Marcus Aurelius reigned jointly with his adoptive brother Lucius Verus for eight years until Verus died. Rather than appoint the most suitable person for his successor as had happened since the time of Nerva, Marcus Aurelius nominated

LEFT Hadrian (117–138) travelled extensively round the Empire during his reign, and did much to consolidate the frontier zones. He was a great admirer of Greek culture and had wide academic and artistic interests. Hadrian was responsible for the construction of an extensive villa at Tivoli near Rome.

his own son Commodus, and ruled jointly with him for three years. During his reign, Barbarians (a Greek term adopted by the Romans) began to break through the northern frontiers.

Commodus succeeded as sole emperor when Marcus Aurelius died in 180, and this marked the turning point of Rome's fortunes. Until then the Roman world was fairly prosperous and relatively at peace, but it was about to collapse into anarchy. Commodus became extremely unpopular in Rome and, after several attempts on his life, he was assassinated in 193. His successor was Publius Helvius Pertinax, a military officer, who was murdered by the Praetorian Guard after only three months and replaced by the senator Didius Julianus. He in turn was ousted by force by Septimius Severus who marched on Rome with his army and took control of the city. For the next few years Severus was involved in conflicts with his rivals until he defeated Clodius Albinus near Lyon in 196.

Septimius Severus came from Leptis Magna in north Africa (now Libya) and spoke Latin with a noticeable foreign accent; the

rulers of the Roman Empire now rarely came from Rome itself. Septimius Severus embarked on generous building programmes, especially at his native city. From 209 he campaigned against the Picts in Britain, but died in York two years later. His sons Geta and Caracalla succeeded him, but Caracalla soon murdered Geta to become sole ruler. One of Caracalla's main actions was to confer citizenship on all free-born men of the empire in a constitution of 212. This was mainly a fiscal measure, since it increased the numbers of people in the empire liable to taxation.

In 217 Caracalla was murdered by his Praetorian Prefect Macrinus who then became emperor, but was himself replaced the following year by Elagabalus. After his murder in 222, Elagabalus' cousin Severus Alexander assumed power, but was also murdered in 235 by the troops who had become disillusioned. His death brought to an end the dynasty of the Severans and marked the beginning of anarchy which was to last for 50 years.

A succession of emperors followed, nearly all of whom met violent deaths in war or conspiracy. The appointment of Diocletian as emperor by the Praetorian Guard in 284 brought an end to this chaos, and the system of administration and government was totally overhauled. Two years later Diocletian made the Empire into a Tetrarchy (four-man rule) led by two *Augusti* (co-emperors) – himself in the east and Maximian in the west. Two *Caesars* (below the rank of *Augusti*) completed the Tetrarchy; these were younger men who would succeed the *Augusti* in due course, and in turn appoint their own *Caesars*. Despite the economic reforms, Diocletian's reign saw a worsening economic situation with chronic inflation and a devalued currency. In 305 Diocletian and Maximian abdicated, bringing an end to the First Tetrarchy.

There followed a period of confusion, but by the early 4th century the old system of the Tetrarchy was restored, with Licinius ruling the east and Constantine the west, each supported by Caesars. In 313, Constantine and Licinius issued a declaration of freedom to worship (the Edict of Milan), which marked the conversion of the Roman Empire to Christianity. Constantine himself became the first emperor to convert to Christianity. At first the emperors managed to rule peacefully

LEFT Septimius Severus (193–211) gained the position of emperor by force after the assassination of Commodus. He was a native of North Africa, and is said to have spoken Latin with a noticeable foreign accent.

together, but from 316 Constantine began to win territory from Licinius and defeated him in 324. Constantine (Flavius Valerius Constantinus, or Constantine the Great) then received the submission of the city of Byzantium (or Constantinople as it was renamed, now Istanbul), and chose it as his new capital. He built a new city there and ruled as sole *Augustus* until his death in 337. The centre of the Roman world had shifted from Rome to the east, and it became a Greek-speaking Christian empire. The old pagan Latin-speaking Roman world with its centre at Rome was now eclipsed.

OPPOSITE PAGE The Emperor Septimius Severus was from Leptis Magna in North Africa. He undertook generous programmes of building, especially in his native city. This theatre at Leptis Magna, though, was built in the 1st–2nd century by another Punic nobleman, Annobal Rufus.

LEFT The tetrarchy or 'four-man rule' of the Empire initiated by the Emperor Diocletian is embodied in this porphyry sculpture representing the four rulers. It was originally looted from Constantinople and taken to Venice, where it is now set into the wall of the cathedral of San Marco.

CHAPTER THREE

SOLDIER
and
CIVILIAN

*Veni, vidi, vici – 'I came, I saw, I
conquered'*
(SUETONIUS, *DIVUS JULIUS*, 37, 2)

THE HOME GUARD

Rome's success in expanding and consolidating its vast Empire depended very much on the army. This became a highly disciplined, well-trained, organized and well-equipped force, using increasingly sophisticated techniques of warfare. However, in the earliest days of the Republic, the army consisted of nothing more than, literally, a 'home guard' – a militia of footsoldiers with a variety of weapons. Private citizens who owned property (mainly the peasantry) were expected to take up arms as volunteers when the need arose. By owning property, they were deemed to have a material interest in protecting the State and, at this stage, there was no need for a permanent army. Men were called up in an emergency and were obliged to provide their own arms and armour. They were paid little more than expenses for their services and were discharged when the emergency was over. Units of seamen were recruited and disbanded in the same way. A pair of consuls was appointed annually to command the army, a quite inefficient method of leadership.

In the early days of Rome, warfare on a massive scale was rare, but gradually the role of the army changed as more territory in Italy was taken over, and the tactics of warfare changed. The richest citizens served in the cavalry, the next wealthiest in the infantry, and the poorest citizens in the navy. The decision to build a network of military roads enabled Rome to undertake its conquest of neighbouring states and others further afield with greater efficiency. A peak came when the Romans defeated King Pyrrhus of Epirus in 275 BC since up to that time the Greeks had been a dominant military force. During the First Punic War Rome rapidly adapted to naval warfare and, despite some severe losses, eventually achieved success.

For the early Republic there are two important descriptions of the Roman army, one written by the Roman historian Livy and the other by the Greek historian Polybius. Livy, who was writing at the time of Augustus, described the army of the 4th century BC, while Polybius wrote about events from 220 BC to 146 BC, although not all of his work has survived.

ARMY REFORMS

Overseas expeditions became very unpopular with the soldiers because they were unwilling to leave home for long periods. The severe disruption to the peasant farmers and the number of casualties they suffered meant that the land was neglected. Small farms were amalgamated into larger estates so that the number of small landowners with a property qualification declined. This decline was also accelerated by the general exodus of people to the towns and so, despite the land reforms of the Gracchi, there was a severe shortage of recruits in the 2nd century BC. Minor reforms of the army took place, but Marius threw recruitment open to Roman citizens without property; as a result, a volunteer force

BELOW A legionary soldier and a horn-blower. The soldier is wearing segmented plate armour and has a helmet and a sword, while the horn-blower wears mail armour.

began to be recruited from the urban poor seeking a career. Instead of being a part-time army, a standing army of full-time professional soldiers was created who signed on for 16 to 20 years. The pay of these legions was raised so that the soldiers could afford to provide their own armour and weapons to a consistent standard, and the soldiers now owed their loyalty to their commanders and not to the State.

Reforms continued so that under Julius Caesar the army had become a highly efficient and professional body. At the end of the civil war in 31 BC, Octavian (Augustus) had several armies under his control, comprising some 60 legions. He therefore decided to rationalize the army, retaining 28 legions (150,000 men) and disbanding the rest. As a result, over 100,000 veterans were settled in colonies, some of which were new foundations. Augustus was also left with 700 warships, out of which he created a permanent navy. As the empire developed and more provinces were acquired, the legions consisted of fewer

ABOVE A mosaic showing a warship with its oars, rigging and boarding plank. The Romans copied Greek and Carthaginian ships, but to compensate for their lack of naval skill they developed a boarding plank with a long iron spike mounted on the prow of the ship. This plank could be dropped on an enemy ship, and the Roman soldiers could fight their way on board.

Italian citizens and more nationalities from outside Italy, resulting in a very cosmopolitan Roman army.

Auxiliary troops were recruited from non-citizens to assist the legions, and initially served in their own areas. They continued to use their own language, were commanded by their own leaders, and used the type of weaponry to which they were traditionally accustomed. From the time of Augustus, auxiliaries numbered 150,000 men and became an integral part of the army. They were no longer allowed to serve in the area from which they were recruited in order to minimize the risk of local revolts.

Due to Augustus' rationalization, the army was now a peacetime force, with its main function being to police new provinces and to defend frontiers. The emperor retained control of *imperium* over provinces in which military units were based, and the Senate was able to select governors for the other provinces. This division of the Empire into imperial and senatorial provinces was an

attempt to keep the soldiers loyal, and they were expected to swear an oath of allegiance to the emperor.

The Praetorian Guard probably came into being as the personal bodyguard of Scipio Aemilianus in the 2nd century BC. It was commanded by a prefect and consisted of nine cohorts, each of 500 to 1,000 men. Only three cohorts were garrisoned in Rome, the others being spread throughout Italy but rarely in the provinces. The Praetorian Guard was an élite force whose soldiers served for 16 years and were paid far more than ordinary legionaries. From time to time, the Guard was involved in the assassination and selection of emperors until it was disbanded by Constantine I.

The upheavals of the 3rd and 4th centuries did much to change the army, and it became more of a mobile force instead of being in permanent garrisons along the frontiers. Army units were placed in cities to defend them against attack as it was no longer possible to defend all the frontier lines (the *limes*).

After the defeat at Adrianople in 378, Rome had to rely increasingly on the uncertain loyalties of the 'federati' or mercenaries.

THE LEGIONS

A legion consisted of about 5,500 highly trained and professional soldiers recruited from Roman citizens. Legionaries served for 25 or 26 years and their pay and conditions were far better than those of auxiliaries. They were not supposed to marry but this regulation was relaxed at the end of the 2nd century.

Each legion was commanded by a legatus, assisted by six military tribunes, and they were all semi-professional soldiers in various stages of their political careers. The *praefectus castrorum* (prefect) was a fully professional officer responsible for the general administration and also for engineering. Below him were 60 centurions (responsible for training and discipline) as well as specialist officers such as surveyors and doctors.

A legion was divided into ten cohorts of 480 men which were in turn divided into six

LEFT Legionary soldiers wearing segmented plate armour and helmets. They are carrying large curved shields and javelins with iron tips and wooden shafts.

ABOVE An auxiliary cavalryman's helmet constructed of bronze and iron dating from the 1st century. This helmet was found near Ely in Cambridgeshire, England.

ABOVE This frieze dating to the 1st century BC shows a battle between Roman and Celtic cavalrymen. A Celtic horse has fallen and has thrown its rider. It is portrayed wearing a saddle with four pommels, a style which was adopted by the Romans.

centuries of 80 men. Within each century there were ten groups of eight men (*contubernia* who shared a tent while on the march or else a pair of barrack rooms. During the Flavian period, the first cohort was almost doubled in size so that it had five centuries of 160 men, while cohorts 2 to 10 each had 480 men. Each century was commanded by a centurion, the most senior of whom was with the First Cohort and was known as the *primus pilus*. Below the centurions, the main officers were called the *principales* and included the standard bearers (*signiferi*).

During the Empire there were usually no more than 28 legions, based mainly along the frontiers. In Republican times, legions were given serial numbers (I, II, III and so on) as they were recruited. After the Civil War, several legions shared the same number, and so they were also given nicknames, such as II *Adiutrix Pia Fidelis*. If a legion was destroyed, disgraced or disbanded, its number was never used again.

THE AUXILIARY UNITS

The auxiliary units were recruited from non-citizens in the provinces to provide specialist skills and additional help for the legions. Auxiliaries served for 25 years, and were composed of either infantry units (*cohortes peditatae*), cavalry units (*alae*), or part-mounted infantry (*cohortes equitatae*). Each *ala* or cohort had 500 men (*quingenaria*) or sometimes 1000 men (*milliaria*).

A cavalry unit was commanded by a prefect and was divided into 16 troops (*turmae*). Each *turma* had about 30 or 40 men and came under the command of a decurion. An infantry cohort was commanded by a prefect and was split into centuries under the command of centurions. The auxiliary units were originally under the leadership of their own native leaders, but this changed during the Empire.

By the end of the 1st century, the auxiliary units had become part of the established regular army, and there was a need to recruit more irregular troops from the frontier zones to make up infantry units (*numeri*) and cavalry units (*cunei*).

THE NAVY

Augustus maintained a professional standing navy which was based very much on the Greek navy, even down to using Greek terminology.

ARMS AND ARMOUR

The equipment used and worn by legionaries was remarkably standard throughout the Empire and there must have been centres for the mass production of equipment. Legionaries wore a linen undergarment under a knee-length, short-sleeved linen tunic. In colder climates, they were allowed to wear leather trousers. Their sandals had very thick leather soles, reinforced with iron hobnails, and were fastened by leather thongs wound halfway up the shin, into which wool or fur could be bound in cold weather.

The early body armour consisted of reinforced leather jerkins or mail shirts of small iron rings, but by the time of Tiberius all the legionaries wore segmented plate armour made of metal strips and plates. This was later replaced by overlapping scale and mail armour. Helmets underwent constant modification from the Republic onwards. The early helmets were usually of bronze, the later ones of iron, and they had a projecting guard at the back to protect the neck. The officers were distinguished by their more elaborate uniforms.

Early legionary shields were oval in shape but in the 1st century they became rectangular, although curved to fit the body. A legionary shield (*scutum*) was made of thin sheets of wood glued together and bound round the edges with wrought iron or bronze. The centre was hollowed out for the hand grip which was protected by a metal boss. The outer surface of the shield was covered with leather on which were fastened decorative bronze plates. Weapons for attack included the *pilum* or javelin, two of which were carried by each man. The pilum was 7 ft (213 cm) long, the top 3 ft (91 cm) being of iron. The sword (*gladius*) was a double-edged weapon about 2 ft (61 cm) long and 2 in (5 cm) wide. Carried in a scabbard attached to a belt on the right-hand side of the body, it was a stabbing rather than a slashing weapon and designed for use in close fighting. The scabbard was usually made of wood and leather held together by bronze. On the left-hand side of the body there was a dagger (*pugio*) in a bronze or iron scabbard suspended from another belt. Daggers seem to have been withdrawn from the legionary armoury by the end of the 1st century.

Legionaries also carried other equipment, including a pickaxe, saw, basket and chain,

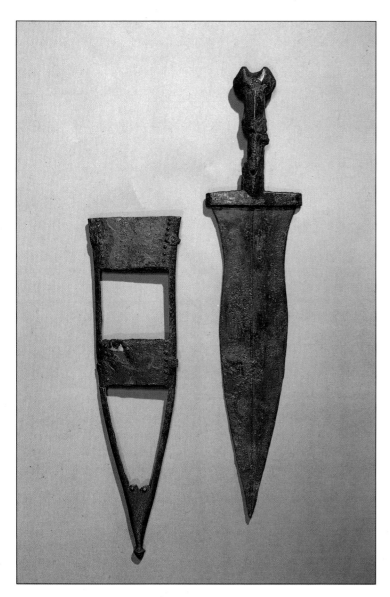

ABOVE
An iron dagger (right) with the iron framework of its scabbard (left), found in London. The dagger was known as a 'pugio', and the scabbard (originally covered in leather or wood) would have been attached to a soldier's belt.

There were three main naval bases, at Misenum (now Miseno) in the Bay of Naples, at Ravenna (now silted up and inshore), and at Forum Julii (now Fréjus in southern France), although the latter base was gradually run down. Augustus subsequently added two fleets for Egypt and Syria, and later on there was a fleet based at Gesoriacum (Boulogne) in northern France for the conquest of Britain in the 1st century. There were also subsidiary fleets on the Rhine, Danube and the Black Sea. The navy was always regarded as an inferior foreign entity and was therefore treated as an auxiliary force. Prefects commanded the imperial fleets, while individual ships were commanded by trierarchs. Ships known as quinqueremes and quadriremes were used, but in the imperial period the trireme was the most common type of warship.

all used in their duties of building camps, and so on. Within the legions the standard-bearers (*signiferi*) were responsible for the legionary standards. These were a distinctive part of army life, being a religious symbol as well as acting as a flag and a rallying point in battles. Loss of the standard was tantamount to disgrace, and could bring about the disbandment of the unit. The standard-bearers wore animal skins over their uniform following an old Celtic practice. In addition to the standards, musical instruments were used to give signals, and these included a type of trumpet and a large curved horn.

There is no standard version of the weaponry of the auxiliaries, as they used and wore the traditional native equipment and armour to which they were accustomed. Some auxiliaries wore no armour, while others (including cavalrymen) wore mail armour or scale armour (rows of overlapping metal scales sewn onto a linen or leather undergarment) as well as helmets. Their shields were usually oval in shape. In the early Empire, horses had no armour, although they did from the time of Hadrian, and the saddle also appeared in the early Empire. The cavalrymen in particular had elaborate parade equipment for themselves and their horses. The infantry used the short sword (*gladius*) as its main weapon, while the cavalry had a longer sword (*spatha*) and an oval or hexagonal flat shield. Specialist units of archers were largely recruited from the eastern provinces.

By the time of Julius Caesar, the Roman army was adept at siege tactics, employing many methods and weapons including battering rams, large catapults to throw heavy rocks, and ballista to fire iron bolts. Only legionaries were allowed to use artillery.

FORTS AND CAMPS

When on campaign, the Roman army normally constructed an enclosure or camp for each overnight stop. The camp was surrounded by a ditch and small rampart with a palisade of sharpened stakes on the top. Inside the camp were rows of leather tents, each of which could house eight men (a *contubernium*). The next day the tent could be rolled up and carried by mule, and the stakes of the palisade were pulled up for re-use elsewhere. The layout of the camps was fairly standard, a playing card shape, but apart from the ditch, very little archaeological evidence survives on such sites and they are often only recognized from aerial photographs. In Republican times, troops were sometimes kept in semi-permanent camps with tents throughout the winter.

Forts were constructed to house troops on a more permanent basis, usually close to or on frontiers. Sites were chosen for their strategic positions and acted as bases for further campaigns and as garrisons for protecting the frontiers. A 'fort' usually housed auxiliary troops or a combined auxiliary and legionary force, while the term 'fortress' was reserved for permanent establishments for a full legion. Information about camps and forts comes from excavated archaeological evidence and from relief sculptures (such as on Trajan's Column). Several classical authors also wrote in detail about military matters, and some Roman military documents have actually survived (such as discharge documents inscribed on pairs of bronze plates). A few were written on papyrus, mainly from Egyptian sites, which was used there for the everyday paperwork of the army, and there are wooden writing tablets which give an insight into routine army life. (A large quantity of these has been found at Vindolanda, near Hadrian's Wall.)

Both the legionary fortresses and the auxiliary forts of the early empire had a very similar layout, although the forts were on a much smaller scale. A fortress occupied an area of about 20 hectares (50 acres), while a fort varied from about 1 to 2.5 hectares (2½ to 6 acres), depending on the type of unit. Forts were very similar, although not identical, right across the empire, and generally they had the same basic street layout.

ABOVE A model of a large catapult used for hurling rocks and stones as part of the artillery used in sieges.

A ROMAN FORT

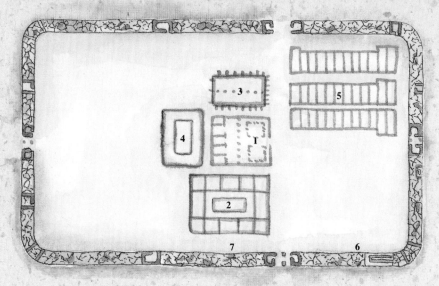

ABOVE An aerial view of Housesteads fort on Hadrian's Wall, which was used by auxiliaries. Some of the excavated buildings are visible including the praetorium, principia, granary, hospital and barracks.

1 Principia
2 Praetorium
3 Granary
4 Hospital
5 Barracks
6 Latrines
7 Rampart

ABOVE *Hadrian's Wall across northern England was part of the defensive frontier initiated by the Emperor Hadrian. It consisted of a stone wall (turf in places) with forts, milecastles and turrets. Similar frontier systems existed elsewhere in the Empire.*

PREVIOUS PAGES
A reconstruction of the fort at London by Alan Sorrell. The infantrymen and cavalrymen are marching toward's the headquarters building, while construction work takes place on their right. In the distance are the ramparts which surround the fort.

The earlier forts were constructed of timber, with ramparts of timber and earth, while later forts were constructed at least partially of stone. They were rectangular in shape with rounded corners ('playing card'), and had four gateways, one in each side. Surrounding the fort were one or more ditches (*fossae*), usually V-shaped with a shallow slot at the bottom. Access to the gates was either by wooden bridges or by earthen causeways across the ditches. The ditches were usually 10–12 ft (300–366 cm) wide at the top and 6–8 ft (185–245 cm) deep. The rampart (*vallum*) inside the ditches was the main barrier; this was usually constructed of upcast material from the ditches on a wooden or stone foundation, and was faced with timber and with turf stacked like bricks to give additional strength and stability. From the 2nd century, stone walls or façades began to be used for ramparts. The gateways had timber towers (later replaced by stone structures) with large reinforced timber doors. There were also corner and interval towers, which in the early Empire did not project beyond the line of the ramparts, but projected internally. The main function of the towers was for the deployment of artillery.

In the centre of the fort, opposite the junction of the two main streets, was the *principia* or headquarters building, the administrative and religious focus of the fort. It was usually a complex of buildings around a courtyard, similar to a civic forum and basilica, and included storerooms, offices, and the shrine (*sacellum*), beneath which was a strong room. The *praetorium* was a spacious residence for the commanding officer, and there were also separate buildings for other officers. Most of the fort was taken up by the soldiers' barracks, which consisted of narrow rectangular buildings fronted by a verandah and divided into a series of rooms with a larger room at one end for officers' (centurions') quarters. Each original tent-party (*contubernium*) of eight men shared a pair of rooms, one for storing equipment and one for sleeping. The men did their own cooking and eating there, since no centralized canteen was provided. Bread, however, was baked in ovens which were located just inside the rampart to minimize the risk of fire. Grain was stored in large granaries (*horrea*) built with a raised floor to give adequate ventilation below and within the building and prevent deterioration of the grain.

Other buildings included workshops, stables and a hospital. The hospital (*valetudinarium*) was usually in a quieter part of the fort, and the army itself was in the forefront of Roman medicine. Considerable measures were taken to ensure an effective medical service, and hygiene was an important factor, with a good water supply and drainage system, including latrines and bath-houses. In a legionary fortress, the bath-house tended to occupy a central position, while in the forts it was often situated in an external annex. The bath-house consisted of a series of rooms of varying temperatures, and provided a social function as well. The amphitheatre, used for entertainment, and probably also for weapon training and parades, was always situated outside forts.

Permanent forts and fortresses invariably led to a sizeable civilian community (*vicus*) growing up outside the fortifications, providing a variety of services.

FRONTIERS

The idea of frontiers did not evolve until the early Roman Empire, when a distinction was made between Roman and non-Roman territory. In many provinces there were natural boundaries, such as a river or the desert. Rome's most serious problems, though, were along its northern boundaries, and the main way of controlling these frontiers was by a system of forts, watchtowers and signal stations.

In Britain, the Emperor Hadrian initiated the building of a human-made barrier of stone and turf, incorporating forts, milecastles and turrets, and now known as Hadrian's Wall. This defensive scheme underwent many modifications, and moved even further north to a new physical barrier in Scotland. This time a turf wall with forts was built, known as the Antonine Wall. A similar frontier system was also developed from the North Sea, along the Rhine and Danube, to the Black Sea and, with other frontiers, is called the *limes*. Along the Rhine and Danube there was a series of forts, watchtowers and signal stations integrated with legionary fortresses. The stretch between the two rivers (from south of Bonn to a point near Regensburg) was defended in a similar way and reinforced by a ditch and palisade, later to be replaced in some sections by a stone wall. In the end, though, this barrier was to prove ineffective against the invading Germanic tribes who overwhelmed the empire.

RETIREMENT

After serving their term in the army, the soldiers were given their discharge and referred

ABOVE The town of Arausio (Orange) in southern Gaul was founded as a colony for veterans in the late 1st century BC. This is a view of the remains of buildings to the west of the theatre, possibly a gymnasium or even an earlier theatre, as well as a large temple with vaults beneath.

RIGHT Part of the unique marble inscription showing the system of centuriation in and around the early colony of Arausio (Orange) in southern Gaul.

to as veterans. Particularly from the time of Augustus, discharge from the army was much better organized and paid for by the state. Auxiliaries were granted citizenship, and proof of the grant was inscribed on a pair of bronze sheets, a diploma, many of which have been found. They received no land, but tended to stay in the country in which they had served.

Legionary veterans were given a cash payment, although in the early Empire they were also given the choice of a grant of land, and were often settled as groups in colonies. Probably in order to ensure that the colonists had control of the surrounding land as well, a system of centuriation was undertaken whereby a large area of countryside was divided into squares owned by the colonists. A unique discovery at Orange in France, founded as a colony for veterans, was the marble fragments of an inscribed plan of the centuriation. This layout is often fossilized in the countryside today, particularly in southern Gaul and Italy, and can be easily recognized in aerial photographs.

CHAPTER FOUR

TOWN HOUSES
and
TENEMENTS

*"When in Rome, live as the
Romans do."*

(ST AMBROSE, 337–397)

THE FIRST TOWNS

In the Mediterranean area, the presence of towns was not new. Greece had for long been a society of city-states, and from the 10th century BC had established colonies as far afield as southern France, southern Italy and Asia Minor. Further east there were oasis towns and caravan cities such as Gerasa (now Jerash in Jordan) and Palmyra (in Syria), while in North Africa the Phoenicians had established successful colonies, as at Carthage (now in Tunisia). In such places, the old native towns were gradually subject to Roman influence and settlement and were sometimes even given a new lease of life. They developed into truly prosperous Roman cities, resulting in a uniformity of appearance right across much of the Empire.

In many parts of the Roman Empire, particularly in areas such as northern Gaul and Britain, cities as such had not previously existed. There had been tribal centres, often situated on hilltops, but although some of these provided a few similar functions, they bore little resemblance to a Roman town. In these areas, the impact of urbanization was dramatic, and it is surprising that these towns became established within a relatively short space of time. In some areas, former tribal capitals became the new towns, controlling a similar administrative district, although they usually moved to a more convenient position away from hilltops. In the northern areas of the Empire, the number of towns remained far fewer than in southern regions such as Italy, which had over 400 Roman towns.

Some new towns developed from deliberate foundations of colonies for veterans, including Colchester in England which was established as a colony in 49 on the site of the former legionary fortress. Other veterans were settled in or near existing towns, as at Pompeii in Italy. Many towns grew up for economic reasons, such as those along trade routes or next to forts, and they often managed to survive even when the army moved on.

TOWN PLANNING

The early towns invariably grew up in a haphazard, unplanned manner, of which Rome itself is a prime example, but new towns became subject to the Greek concept of town planning. From the 1st century BC almost

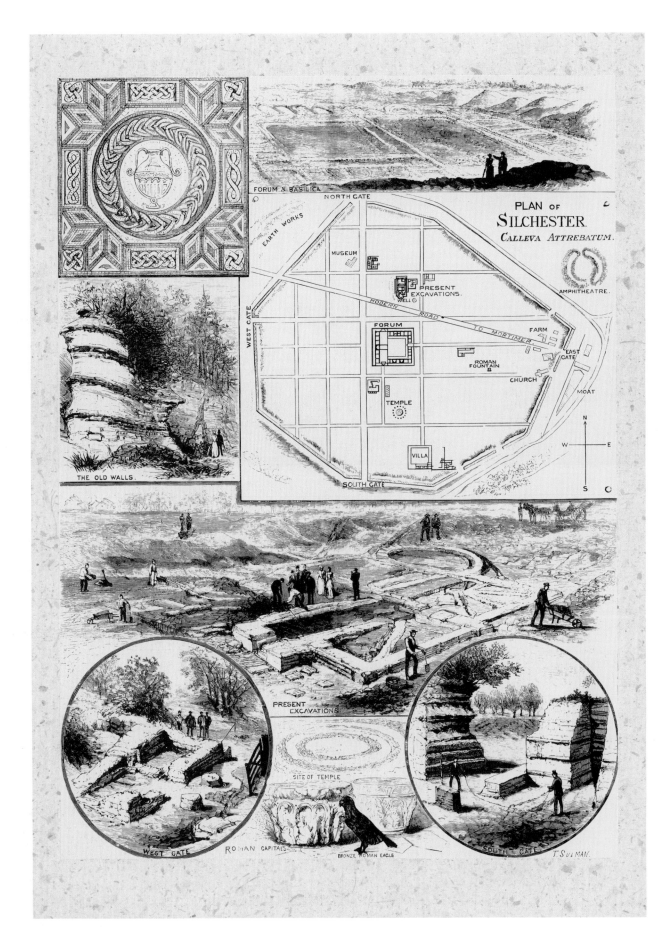

FORUM & BASILICA

PLAN of
SILCHESTER.
CALLEVA ATTREBATUM.

NORTH GATE

EARTH WORKS

MUSEUM

AMPHITHEATRE.

PRESENT
EXCAVATIONS.

WELL

WEST GATE

MODERN ROAD TO MORTIMER

FARM

FORUM

EAST GATE

ROMAN
FOUNTAIN

CHURCH

MOAT

TEMPLE

VILLA

N
W E
S

SOUTH GATE

THE OLD WALLS.

PRESENT
EXCAVATIONS

SITE OF TEMPLE

WEST GATE

ROMAN CAPITALS

BRONZE ROMAN EAGLE

SOUTH GATE

T. SULMAN.

every new colony was planned on a grid system resembling the layout of a fort, while existing towns such as Palmyra retained their irregular plan, but grew in size. The population of towns varied considerably, but by Caesar's time Rome is thought to have had a population of a million.

Over the years many towns were endowed with fine buildings by imperial and private benefactors, the latter usually in an attempt to advance their political careers or enhance their prestige. The period from the Flavian to the Severan emperors was particularly prosperous for towns. Much of the architecture was influenced by Greek building techniques and styles, especially in the design of theatres and basilicas. In the 3rd century BC, though, a revolutionary technique of building completely changed methods of construction and influenced architectural design. This was the use of concrete, which was employed in conjunction with the arch (which had never been fully exploited by the Greeks), so that vast new building complexes could be constructed. This in turn led to the development of the barrel vault, which was a particular feature of the roofs of bath-houses.

ABOVE A reconstruction by Ronald Embleton of the forum at London, with a basilica on the far side and offices and colonnaded walkways on the other three sides. The open square is being used as a market.

OPPOSITE PAGE New towns such as Silchester in England were laid out on a grid plan similar to that of forts, with the forum occupying the position of the principia in a fort. The site was extensively excavated in the 19th century, without the benefit of modern techniques.

PUBLIC BUILDINGS

Apart from bath-houses, the public buildings in a town often included an amphitheatre, theatre, circus, forum, and temples, as well as other amenities and structures such as aqueducts, sewers and latrines. A town could also have its status enhanced by the provision of town walls (although these were subsequently erected for defensive purposes) and also by monumental arches. The Romans built these to commemorate various events, particularly at the entrances to provincial towns as an expression of civic pride. Such arches were frequently built to mark the foundation of the town and the exploits of the veterans settling there, and they could be either free-standing or built into the town walls.

The forum was the civic centre, used for administration, trade and as a meeting place. In the Republic they tended to be irregularly shaped un-enclosed areas, but subsequently they were surrounded by offices, colonnaded walks, and an aisled building known as the basilica. In Britain they usually had colonnades on three sides and a basilica on the fourth side, resembling the army headquarters

LEFT *The 'Hunting Baths' on the outskirts of Leptis Magna in North Africa. They survived virtually intact beneath the sand dunes. Inside a wall painting depicting hunting scenes suggests that the baths were owned by a company of hunters who provided wild animals for use in amphitheatres.*

(*principia*) of a fort. There was sometimes a *cryptoporticus* beneath the forum, as at Arles in France. This was a series of underground passageways, possibly used as a meeting place, as storerooms, or even as barracks to house the public slaves of the town.

A forum could act as a market place, but some towns had purpose-built markets, the most ambitious being Trajan's Market in Rome, a vast complex of markets, libraries, a forum and a basilica overlooking Trajan's Column. Most shops in towns were open-fronted, many with goods and food being made on the premises in full public view. Traders could also operate from street stalls, which often caused great congestion.

Public baths (run by the state or by private companies) did not become common in the early towns until the 1st century BC, but most towns came to possess at least one public bath building. They were very much linked with the provision of water from aqueducts. The four main rooms were the undressing room (*apodyterium*), the cold room (*frigidarium*), the warm room (*tepidarium*) and the hot room (*caldarium*), but more sophisticated establishments had cold plunge baths, a very hot sweating room, exercise rooms, courtyards and covered walks. The source of heat for early baths was a charcoal brazier, but by the 1st century BC a system of underfloor heating (hypocaust) was used. Bathing estab-

lishments were a social focus of the city and became extremely popular; by the 4th century there were nearly 1,000 establishments in Rome itself. The practice of mixed bathing was forbidden in a decree by Hadrian in the 2nd century, and where separate facilities were not available, the sessions for men and women had to be split, with women bathing in the morning.

THE WATER SUPPLY

An adequate water supply was essential for town life, and in the early towns water was taken from wells and springs, but with a rising population this system rapidly became inadequate. The first known aqueduct at Rome dates from the 4th century BC, and a system of aqueducts soon supplied many towns throughout the Empire. Many aqueducts consisted of simple channels dug into the ground, as well as underground wood, terracotta or lead pipes. The most imposing method of water supply, though, was the overground aqueducts supported on arches, the first one being built in Rome in the 2nd century BC. Some 300 years later, ten main aqueducts were supplying Rome with water.

The overground aqueducts sometimes had to cross steep gorges and travel through hillsides in tunnels. The gradient of the masonry conduits had to be carefully controlled, and the engineering and surveying of aqueducts

DISTRIBUTION OF WATER

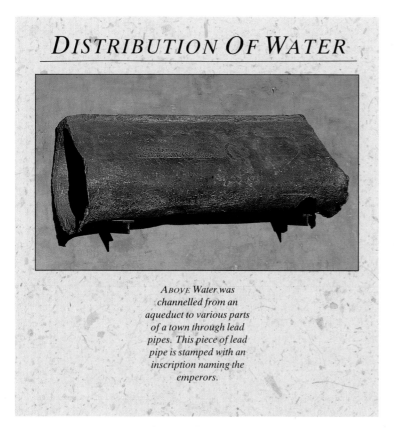

ABOVE Water was channelled from an aqueduct to various parts of a town through lead pipes. This piece of lead pipe is stamped with an inscription naming the emperors.

was very precise. Once built, they only required routine cleaning and maintenance; at Segovia in Spain the aqueduct is still in working order. The top of the channel on overground aqueducts was sealed to prevent evaporation and contamination, and yet the channel had to be sufficiently large to enable repairs and cleaning to be carried out. One aqueduct serving Nîmes (in France) was partly in a channel, partly in a tunnel, and partly on low arches, and crossed the River Gard on a huge bridge known today as the Pont du Gard. The bridge was 1542 ft (470 m) long and 161 ft (49 m) high, and is the highest surviving bridge structure from the Roman world. It was built in the late 1st century BC and ran for 31 miles (50 km), with a flow of 1,059,300 cubic feet (30,000 cubic metres) of water per day. This aqueduct is still an impressive sight.

Once in the towns, the water was distributed in lead, terracotta or timber pipes to the various baths, public fountains and rich private houses – only a few homes could afford piped water. In Nîmes, the circular distribution settling tank at the end of the aqueduct still survives. From this, large lead pipes carried water to various parts of the town.

With such a quantity of water coming into the towns in aqueducts, and no system of controlling or stopping the flow, an efficient drainage system was essential. The drainage system could consist of substantial masonry sewers or timber-lined drains. The public latrines, usually flushed by water from the baths, often had a series of seats in a row, and it appears that there were no inhibitions in sitting alongside other people.

DOMESTIC HOUSES

Town houses could be very luxurious, with a central hall (*atrium*) opening on to a colonnaded courtyard or garden. Such houses had a variety of rooms, some including a bath suite, and there is evidence of upper storeys. The houses were decorated with fine mosaics, wall paintings, sculptures, and an elaborate range of furniture, and some had glazed windows as well.

Conversely, most of the population lived in far more humble dwellings. In 4th-century catalogues about Rome, only 1,790 of the sole-family type of residence were recorded, but there were 46,000 tenement blocks, each inhabited by many families. The urban poor mostly lived in these badly constructed buildings, which were prone to gross overcrowding, collapse, fire and epidemics, as well as ever-rising rents. Eventually, a height limit of 60 ft (20 metres) was imposed on tenement blocks, along with improved building regulations to prevent collapse and the spread of fire.

In the northern empire, tenement blocks were unusual, and instead the poor lived in small rows of timber houses, sometimes incorporating shops which fronted on to the streets. For most people, towns were extremely cramped, dirty and noisy places, both day and night – in Rome, for example, carts were only allowed to pass through the streets at night. Juvenal, the satirist, writing in Rome at the end of the 1st century AD, noted that 'in this city, sleep comes only to the wealthy'.

RICH AND POOR

Society was rigorously stratified by wealth and by law, and so there was a huge disparity between rich and poor, free citizens, non-citizens and slaves. Most of the written and archaeological evidence originates from the wealthier classes, who included senators, knights and magistrates. The poorer classes – citizens and non-citizens – made up a large proportion of the population. Women, al-

LEFT The covered channel of an aqueduct had to be large enough for a person to carry out repairs and cleaning. Some of the covering slabs are missing from this channel at the Pont du Gard, which is at a height of 151 ft (49 m) above the river.

RIGHT In the town, the aqueduct would usually terminate in a settling tank from which numerous pipes distributed the water to various parts of the town. This example still survives at Nîmes in southern France, and the holes for the lead pipes can be seen.

RIGHT Public latrines consisted of one or more rows of seats over a drain which was usually flushed by water from the baths. The channel in front was for cleaning the sponges on sticks used for personal hygiene. There seem to have been no concerns about privacy.

HOUSING FOR THE POOR

ABOVE A model of a substantial tenement block at the port of Ostia near Rome. They were lived in by the poor, and were usually badly constructed and prone to collapse and fire.

though possessing some rights, including ownership of property, tended to play a role defined and determined by the rights assigned to them by men.

In the 1st century, slaves represented up to one third of the urban population. They were employed extensively in a variety of ways, such as in the building and maintenance of roads and aqueducts, as domestic servants (often an educated Greek slave acting as a tutor), as factory workers and as gladiators and prostitutes. Wealthy private households might own numerous slaves. The treatment of slaves varied considerably depending on their owners; many were subject to brutality, even though the Roman economy depended on slaves.

The majority of people in the towns spent their day working to earn money to support their families, with only a few wealthy people living off their investments. Many small manufacturing trades were carried out in towns, although heavier industries were usually sited outside. Small shops and stalls sold food and other goods and services, while many workers were employed in the docks or as porters in the markets. There was plenty of entertainment, including circuses, amphitheatres, and theatres. In times of crises the towns themselves, particularly those with defensive walls, could act as places of refuge. In general, towns were noisy, dirty, bustling, crowded places but, despite all the activity, most towns depended directly on agriculture for their wealth and for food supply. In contrast to many modern towns, Roman towns were an integral part of the surrounding countryside.

CHAPTER FIVE

COTTAGES
and
COUNTRY HOUSES

'*Friends, Romans, countrymen*'
**(WILLIAM SHAKESPEARE, *JULIUS CAESAR*,
ACT III, Sc. ii, 79)**

THE DEMISE OF THE PEASANT

The very first villages of Rome were farming villages, and in the early Republic there were many peasant farmers in Italy who were ready to take up arms to defend their land. However, this duty became too burdensome and, after the Punic Wars, many families were no longer able to work their land, which had been neglected after so many years of military campaigning. Debts were incurred, farms were sold, and the dispossessed peasants flocked to the towns to add to the increasing numbers of urban poor. In the meantime, the rich, who had profited from the wars, bought up large tracts of land, replacing the small landholdings with large estates (*latifundia*), which they ran as absentee landlords, a situation which was never substantially improved even with subsequent land reforms.

Apart from wealthy speculators, the peasants were also dispossessed by colonies of veterans who were granted land on their discharge from the army. The land was often divided into regular units, a system known as centuriation, and the resulting pattern of fields is fossilized in many areas today. It is particularly noticeable on aerial photographs in Northern Italy around the Po Valley.

SLAVERY

The large estates (*latifundia*) were worked by slaves, in plentiful supply following each military victory. *Latifundia* spread to the provinces, although they were probably not as common there as in Italy, and there is some evidence for the use of slaves in the provinces as well. Slavery was not an innovation; many of the northern Celtic tribes, such as those in

ABOVE Most slaves died without leaving any trace, but Junius is remembered in this mosaic. He was obviously a slave who worked indoors.

Britain, had previously traded in slaves with Rome.

Most slaves died without leaving any trace of their existence. On farms especially, their treatment could be quite harsh and in the 2nd century BC there were two slave revolts in Sicily. Soon afterwards, the final and biggest slave revolt in antiquity took place under

RIGHT A chained Gaulish warrior who has been captured by the Romans. Most captives were sold into slavery.

LEFT Centuriation was a method of dividing the land into regular units for allotment to veteran soldiers. This marble inscription shows part of the original layout at Orange in France. Many peasants were dispossessed as a result of veteran soldiers being granted their land.

ABOVE A rural scene from a wall painting in the villa of Agrippa Postumus at Boscotrecase near Pompeii.

the leadership of Spartacus, a gladiator. In 73 BC he escaped and assembled a force of fugitives on Mount Vesuvius, eventually forming an army of tens of thousands of slaves. For two years they wandered throughout Italy, pillaging and plundering, until they were eventually defeated by the Roman army under Crassus. Following this defeat, over 6,000 captured slaves were crucified along the Appian Way, the road leading from Rome to Capua.

THE GROWTH OF THE VILLAS

Villas began to appear in the provinces from the 1st century BC, and in many areas the villa system did not go out of use for 500 years. It extended right across the Empire, from Britain to the Sahara, in diverse geographical areas. Like other aspects of Roman life, it is difficult to generalize about villas, but they had much more in common with the great country houses and plantations of 18th and 19th century Europe and America than with the more humble and utilitarian types of farming establishment.

In Italy and elsewhere, the native population that continued to farm the land gradually adopted Roman styles of living. There is evidence that Roman types of housing and fur-

ABOVE Much information about villas and agriculture can be obtained from mosaics. This one shows a large 4th-century estate in Tunisia, with the villa buildings and bath-house in the centre, surrounded by agricultural activity throughout the four seasons.

nishing were in such demand that huge debts were incurred to pay for them. The poorer farmers rented small farms and homesteads, while the more wealthy farmers lived in what are termed 'villas' – large farming estates with domestic buildings often decorated with mosaics and wall paintings, and displaying other signs of Roman influence. It used to be thought that all villas in the provinces were owned and lived in by Romans who had moved there from Italy. Except possibly for a few of the very large villas, the builders and owners of the provincial villas were probably natives, although their names are rarely recorded.

Villas were more common in the northern provinces, and examples in northern Gaul were often very extensive. Some villas clustered around towns and were used as country retreats within easy reach of the towns by their wealthy owners. A few villas were associated with industry rather than with agriculture.

The information we have about villas comes from archaeological excavations and aerial photography. Villas were sometimes represented in art, usually in wall paintings and mosaics (especially mosaics from North Africa), and ancient authors also wrote about

agriculture and villa buildings. Marcus Porcius Cato, writing in the first half of the 2nd century BC, described how to run one of the large new estates with slaves in his book *De Agri Cultura (On Agriculture)*. Place-names can often give clues to the existence of a villa – 'Ville Rouge' in France, for example, may indicate past discoveries of Roman tiles from a villa. Place-names of original Roman estates can also survive, or at least be traced in early medieval documents.

THE APPEARANCE OF THE VILLAS

The villa buildings were usually quite different from anything else previously seen in the provinces; places like Britain took rather longer to incorporate Roman features than some of the Mediterranean provinces. Even so, the early villas with their simple rectangular timber buildings divided into rooms and adorned with mosaics, wall paintings and tiled roofs were very different from the circular wattle and daub huts with thatched

ABOVE A reconstruction of a Roman kitchen. In the far corner is an oven, and stored in the kitchen are pottery vessels including amphorae, metal strainers, a quernstone, and glass bottles.

roofs common in Britain before the Roman invasion.

The more prosperous villas had various features such as glazed windows, tiled roofs, mosaics, plastered and painted walls, under-floor heating, and bath-houses. Mosaics were mainly used for floors and were made from thousands of tiny cubes (*tessellae*), usually of stone, tile, glass fragments and pottery, forming either a simple pattern or a more complex scene, such as one from Greek or Roman mythology. Decorated walls were usually covered in two or three layers of plaster and then the outline of a design would be sketched or scratched on the surface. The painting could then be done in a wide range of colours.

In colder climates, rooms could be heated by charcoal braziers, but the development of underfloor heating (hypocausts), like that used in bath-houses, provided a more efficient form of heating. Hot air from a furnace passed through the air space beneath the floor, with gases and heat escaping through flues in the walls. The floor was usually sup-

HYPOCAUST HEATING

LEFT These stacks of tiles supported a floor as part of the system of underfloor heating in one room of the villa. The hot air circulated beneath the floor.

ported on stacks of tiles or stone, or else the hot air circulated through stone-lined channels beneath the floor. This system of heating was usually only employed in a small proportion of ground-floor rooms.

RIGHT A mosaic floor depicting the treading of grapes for the manufacture of wine.

AGRICULTURE

The type of agriculture carried out depended very much on the geographical region. From the late Republic methods of agriculture improved, although vast technological changes never took place, probably because of the reliance on cheap labour. Italy was initially fairly self-sufficient and even exported quantities of wine as far afield as Britain. For a time, olive and vine production was illegal elsewhere in order to safeguard Italy's interests and to ensure that other regions concentrated on the production of cereals which could be imported for the inhabitants of Rome.

As increasing numbers of people moved to Rome, its huge population needed more food. Under Roman rule, North Africa be-

came immensely productive, with its agriculture supported by sophisticated irrigation systems. As in Italy, estates became very large and grain was their major product, with Africa and Egypt especially supplying two-thirds of Rome's needs. By the 2nd century wine and olive oil exports from North Africa became important as well, and the distinctive and durable remains of the olive presses have enabled olive-growing areas to be mapped and have provided evidence of the thousands of small farms and villas which grew olives.

In the northern provinces, where olives and vines could not be cultivated, livestock rearing was important as well as cereals and market gardening.

Farming in these areas was improved by a more efficient type of plough, by improvements in tools, including large two-handled scythes, and by the use of corn-drying ovens. These ovens have often been found on villa sites, along with a range of other outbuildings such as barns and smithies.

Surplus produce in the Roman period could be much more easily transported with the improved communication system, and the increased taxes and levies may initially, at least, have stimulated agricultural production throughout the Empire.

AGRICULTURE DECLINE

In the 3rd century there was economic collapse within the Empire and invasion from beyond the frontiers, and therefore a consequent reduction in the production of manufactured goods and agriculture. Land was left uncultivated and farms were abandoned. For some of the peasant population, life was so difficult in the 3rd century that they took to brigandage, often joining groups of Germanic tribespeople. The name *Bagaudae* appears in the late 3rd century to describe these people. There is evidence of decay and destruction in most villa sites of this period, and a general lowering of standards in areas away from the frontiers, but from the 4th century there was a recovery, although hardly ever matching the previous prosperity. In some areas, the

troubles in the 3rd century led to a complete collapse of the villa system.

The situation in Britain was somewhat different because during the 3rd century there was a recession rather than abandonment and destruction. Instead of a modest recovery, there was a considerable increase in prosperity in the late 3rd and 4th centuries, with new villas being built and existing ones enlarged. There is some evidence for immigration by Gaulish landowners seeking refuge from the troubles. Towards the end of the 4th century villa buildings in Britain declined and were largely abandoned, and many villas elsewhere failed to survive beyond the Roman period. Likewise, many areas went out of agricultural use, such as in North Africa where thousands of acres of arable land were

lost in the 5th century as a result of the failure to maintain the water irrigation systems.

LIFE EXPECTANCY

No matter where people lived, in towns or the countryside, social and economic factors affected both longevity and the quality of life. The infant mortality rate was high, and most working-class people died between the ages of 35 and 50; many people did not live beyond their 20s and 30s. Girls often married in their early teens and could be grandmothers by the age of 30. Inevitably, the wealthier classes had a better chance of living longer. The Emperor Tiberius, for example, was 79 when he died, but on the whole living to what is nowadays considered to be an advanced age was most unusual.

ABOVE The stone relief from a Roman sarcophagus depicts two women bathing a baby.

CHAPTER SIX

GAMES
and
GATHERINGS

*'Hail Emperor, those about to
die salute you'*
(SUETONIUS, *CLAUDIUS*, 21)

PRIVATE ENTERTAINMENT

As in any society, the Romans spent their leisure hours in a variety of ways. In Roman art children are portrayed playing traditional games like hide-and-seek and leap-frog, and are also seen accompanied by their pets. Various toys have been found including dolls made of wood, bone, baked clay and cloth, although it is not always possible to be certain if miniature carvings (such as animals) were toys or votive offerings to a god. Board games were also played, probably by children and adults alike, and gambling and dicing became widespread pursuits throughout the empire. Boards divided into squares have been found, as well as counters (usually made of bone, baked clay or glass) and quantities of bone dice with a series of incised circles on each side. Loaded dice have also been found, showing that not everyone played fair. The playing of knucklebones was also a favourite game.

People of all social classes spent time at the baths and this became a recreational activity. Another form of private entertainment was eating and drinking, which for the poorer classes usually meant frequenting the numerous local taverns. These were undoubtedly of varying reputation, and could also be

ABOVE The playing of knucklebones was a favourite game with men and women.

BELOW An antiquarian painting showing a hunting scene on a mosaic from a villa at East Coker in Somerset. The two hunters with spears are carrying home a doe hung on a pole.

used as gaming houses. At Pompeii, over 100 taverns have been identified, several functioning as brothels as well, with unsettled accounts still marked on the walls.

The wealthy had the money and facilities for private entertaining, from modest dinner parties to lavish banquets. These are a common topic in the contemporary literature which has therefore given much information about details such as food, after-dinner entertainment and difficult guests. Many

MUSICAL ENTERTAINMENT

ABOVE Music was a minor form of entertainment in the Roman period. It was used particularly as an accompaniment to other types of entertainment in theatres and amphitheatres. This 1st century mosiac by Dioscurides portrays a scene from a comedy.

BELOW The poet Virgil (centre) was responsible for some of the greatest works of Latin literature. He is portrayed writing the Aeneid, *flanked by two muses.*

recipes have survived in a cookery book supposed to have been written by the gourmet Apicius in the 1st century. Hunting and fishing added welcome variety to the Roman diet.

Most Romans ate three meals a day, with the main meal being in the early evening. It is likely that the urban poor mainly ate a type of porridge made from boiled wheat, or else bread (if they had an oven for baking). There was a variety of other foods, including meat, cheese, vegetables, nuts, shellfish and fruit, many available only to the wealthier classes. Information about food is obtained from literary sources, art (such as mosaics) and archaeological excavations, where even the pips of different fruit can be identified. One of the most popular ingredients in Roman cooking was a fish sauce called *garum* or *liquamen*, which was widely traded and usually transported in *amphorae* (large pottery jars with a rounded or pointed bottom).

LITERATURE AND MUSIC

After-dinner entertainment could often include discussion and recitation of literature. Latin literature began in the 3rd century BC, with comedies written in verse by Plautus. These, like those written by Terence in the 160s BC, were based on earlier Greek comedies. Latin literature developed during the Republic, and among its greatest works were those of Virgil, Horace and Ovid in the Augustan age. Very little drama was written, but accounts of history became popular in the early Empire. At first poets were considered to be of a low status, but there was a shift in attitude towards poetry in the late Republic, and poets began to live by patronage, offering their patrons a chance of immortality. The reading aloud of literary works took place at private functions and also at recitations; it was, nevertheless, a pastime confined to a minority of educated people.

ABOVE The theatre at the town of Orange in France is typical of Roman-style theatres, with seats surrounding an orchestra, a stage, and a back wall (scaena). A statue of Augustus looks down upon the scene.

Most literature was recorded with pen and ink on papyrus or parchment. Copies of works were laboriously made by hand, and yet many cities had one or more libraries.

Music played a minor part in recreation, and it was not as highly regarded as it had been by the Greeks. Most musical instruments were played to accompany public games and religious rites, and to act as signals in the army. Several types of wind, string and percussion instruments are known, and even a hydraulic organ was developed, but there is very little evidence of the type of music played. Only a few examples have been found of the *odeum*, a small permanently roofed theatre specifically for musical performances and recitations.

PUBLIC GAMES

Roman society was bound up in religious festivals which included public games, but gra-

ABOVE
A mosaic from the 'Room of the Ten Girls' in the 3rd-century villa at Piazza Armerina, Sicily, shows female acrobats and dancers wearing black bikinis, possibly made of leather.

RIGHT Although very similar in design to those worn in the mosaic above, these trunks are over a hundred years older and are perhaps the oldest example of bikini wear yet found. Surprisingly these trunks were not found in the warmer climes of Rome or Greece, but in a 1st-century well in London. The original hip measurement of the wearer has been calculated as approximately 31 inches (79 cm).

dually the religious significance of the games was lost although the games continued to be held regularly. In the mid-4th century BC, games only lasted one day a year, but this increased to several days and by the late Republic, 17 days in the year were devoted to them. In the 1st century BC private games were initiated by military leaders to celebrate personal military victories, and these became so lavish that the distinction between private and official games was hardly discernible.

The emperors continued this tradition of games as it was a means of obtaining popular support and of controlling the activities of the urban masses. Like subsidized food, the games were soon regarded as a right and, according to Juvenal, the populace was only interested in *panem et circenses* – bread and circuses. Colossal sums of public and private money were spent on the games and each of the emperors attempted to outdo his predecessor. The number of official celebrations increased, reaching 135 by the end of the 2nd century, and 176 by the 4th century. In addition, there were special celebrations such as the one for Trajan's victory over the Dacians, with the games lasting for over 100 days. Most people worked for a living but nevertheless found some time to attend the games.

Three types of mass entertainment emerged – gladiatorial combats in amphitheatres, chariot races in circuses, and performances in the theatre and odeum. The events had their origins in Etruscan funerary rites and in

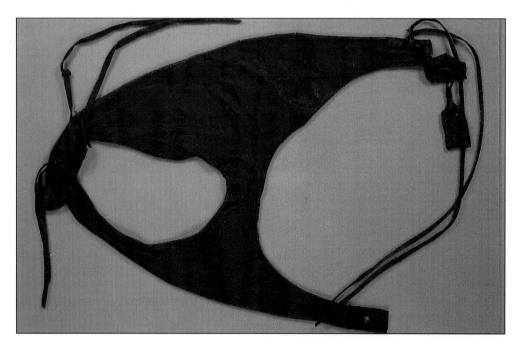

ABOVE Actors in their masks about to perform in a theatrical production.

Greek theatre but became significantly modified to satisfy the demands of the Roman populace, and were often of a sadistic nature.

In imperial times, Greek sports were included in the public games, and emperors tried to revive the glory of the Olympic Games which had waned after the Roman conquest of Greece. Few Romans themselves took part in this type of sporting activity, but in the 1st to 3rd centuries the Games did take place once more at Olympia, and similar events were staged in Italy. Nero went to Greece in 67 to compete in the national festivals, and such was his influence that he returned with 1,808 first prizes including prizes from the Olympic Games!

THEATRES

Under Greek influence, theatrical performances (*ludi scaenici*) became popular from the 2nd century BC, although the Greek tradition of theatre died out. Up to the end of the Republic, performances were produced in improvised wooden buildings which were dismantled afterwards. Permanent theatres began to be constructed, consisting of an auditorium with curved rows of seats rising in tiers, an arena or orchestra, a raised stage, and elaborate stage buildings behind. The theatre was usually unroofed, but could be protected from the weather by awnings.

Theatrical performances of Greek tragedies and comedies were popular with the educated social classes. No women were allowed on stage, and so actors wore masks to distinguish clearly their various roles, male or female. However, the few plays that seem to have been written by Roman authors were intended to be read aloud to a small audience rather than for actual theatrical productions.

Most of the public preferred less taxing entertainment, and from the 1st century BC pantomime and mime became popular, but still usually with mythological themes. In pantomimes the actors mimed their roles, accompanied by music, singing, dancing and elaborate visual effects so that the production was similar to an extravagant ballet. In mime the actors had speaking parts. Women were allowed to take part in mime and pantomime, and these events degenerated into extremely popular, vulgar and tasteless shows.

THE AMPHITHEATRE

ABOVE *Amphitheatres could be substantial stone structures, requiring a great deal of labour and engineering skill in their construction.*

AMPHITHEATRES

The amphitheatre was an oval arena surrounded by tiers of seats. It probably originated in Campania, with one of the earliest being at Pompeii. Some were associated with military forts and Rome's earliest stone amphitheatre was built in 29 BC. By the 2nd century few towns in the western provinces and North Africa were without an amphitheatre. While some were fairly simply built, with seats set into banks of earth, others were very elaborate stone structures. Five amphitheatres were built in Rome, the largest being the Colosseum (properly called the Flavian amphitheatre) which could accommodate 50,000 spectators. Below the arena floor was a complex system of underground passages and rooms for the gladiators and wild animals, as well as machinery which enabled the scenery of the arena to be changed. There was also an intricate water system for converting the arena into a lake for naval battles (*naumachia*). Like the theatre, admission to the amphitheatre was free.

One of the most popular forms of entertainment was the gladiatorial combat – a fight for life between two gladiators. This type of performance dated back to Etruscan times and often accompanied the death of a chieftain. In Rome, the earliest recorded perfor-

A cut–away view through an amphitheatre showing the complex system of arches, vaults, staircases and passages.

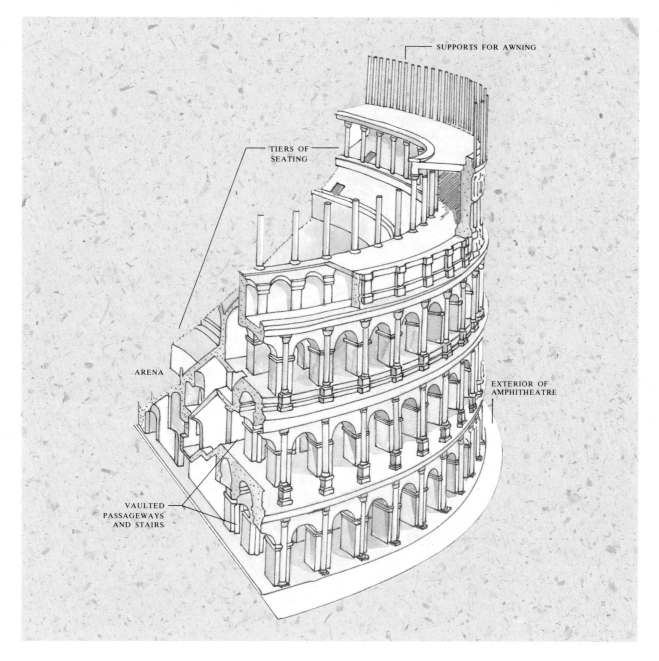

SUPPORTS FOR AWNING

TIERS OF SEATING

ARENA

EXTERIOR OF AMPHITHEATRE

VAULTED PASSAGEWAYS AND STAIRS

71

RIGHT A riot taking place between the inhabitants of Pompeii and visitors from Nuceria during games at the amphitheatre. This incident is actually recorded in Roman history, and led to the closure of the amphitheatre for several years. This wall painting also shows awnings in use at the amphitheatre.

mance was at the funeral of a nobleman in 264 BC. By the 1st century BC these contests had lost their ritual significance and had become spectacles of entertainment, with slaves being made to fight as gladiators since their lives were considered to be of no value.

Gladiatorial training schools were set up and owned by military leaders; Caesar owned a school of 5,000 gladiators. In the 1st century the schools came under state control, removing the danger of them becoming personal armies. As well as trainers, the schools employed numerous other specialists including doctors, and at any one time they could offer the services of thousands of gladiators, mostly slaves. The gladiators were housed in barracks at the schools and trained in various modes of fighting. The type of fighting was based on different native methods using national weapons; particularly favoured were the *retiarii* (net fighters) who used a net to catch their opponents and a trident or dagger to kill them.

The gladiatorial games were not part of the public games (*ludi*) but were called *munera* (duties or obligations) because of the original duty of honouring the dead with such displays. The number of contests grew

rapidly, and in 65 BC Julius Caesar arranged a contest between 320 pairs of gladiators. Hundreds of thousands of gladiators must have lost their lives, although successful fighters could win much popularity and their freedom.

Games using animals (*venationes*) were based on the hunt and became very popular. *Bestiarii* were gladiators who hunted and fought wild animals on foot, and were armed with bows and arrows, although cavalry hunters were sometimes used. The animals used included bears, lions, tigers, panthers, rhinoceroses, leopards, elephants and wild bulls. Bull fights were introduced from Thessaly where they had featured in religious festivals, and bull fighting today is sometimes staged in restored Roman amphitheatres. Animals were also set against each other, such as an elephant against a bear, and the technical apparatus of the arena allowed spectacular stage sets to be used, into which the animals were let loose.

A large trade grew up with frontier provinces and beyond (particularly with Africa), to provide the exotic animals needed for the

ABOVE A fragmentary mosaic from Tunisia showing a chariot race in action, with the chariots going anti-clockwise round the spina. The audience watches the entertainment from the raised seating of the circus.

games. Hunters trapped the animals in pits or drove them into nets or enclosures, and the captured animals were transported in wooden crates with sliding doors, carried on poles by the hunter. They were then transferred to carts pulled by oxen and taken by boat to their final destination. These scenes are sometimes represented on mosaics, as at the Piazza Armerina in Sicily. The carnage of animals reached massive proportions. During Nero's reign, 400 bears and 300 lions were killed on a single occasion; during the inauguration of the Colosseum, in 80, some 9,000 animals are said to have been killed.

In addition to the slaughter of animals for entertainment, there were also well-trained animals which gave circus-like performances, often accompanied by music, which was an important feature of the games. Musicians amused the audience during intervals and announced and accompanied the different spectacles.

The morning of the games was originally reserved for fights with wild animals, midday for executions, and the afternoon for gladiatorial contests, but the divisions became less

RIGHT Romans frequently removed obelisks from Egypt for use as markers in circuses. This one at Arles in France was originally part of the spina of the circus, but in 1675 during the reign of Louis XIV it was set up on a monumental pedestal in the centre of a fountain.

distinct. As well as being victims, animals were also used as executioners of criminals and of enemies of the state (including Jews and Christians) who were condemned to die by animals (*ad bestias*). Methods of killing animals and criminals were ingenious and few people in Rome condemned these spectacles which today most people would find abhorrent.

CIRCUSES

Chariot racing was the oldest and most popular sport in the Roman world. Circus games (*ludi circenses*) were of Etruscan origin and the earliest ones in Rome consisted of chariot races and boxing matches. In the early 2nd century BC, Greek athletics and wrestling entered the games, but it was chariot racing that became the foremost entertainment.

According to Roman legend, the first chariot racing event was arranged by Romulus soon after he founded Rome in 753 BC. He invited the men of the neighbouring Sabine tribe to attend, and while they were engrossed in the games, the women were abducted. The first Etruscan king, Tarquinius Priscus, had a sports ground prepared in the centre of Rome, which was later replaced by the Circus Maximus. In 221 BC the Circus Flaminius was also constructed, and by the 3rd century there were eight tracks in the vicinity of Rome and many more throughout the empire. No circuses have been positively identified in Britain, but chariot racing could take place wherever there was a suitable flat area, with a nearby hillside for spectators.

In Rome and other cities the circuses consisted of a long racetrack flanked by tiers of seats. There were two long parallel sides and rounded ends, the seats being either of stone or built into the sloping hillsides. A low wall (*spina*) ran down the centre of the track, preventing head-on collisions, and there were markers at each end. Some of the circuses were colossal structures – the Circus Maximus at Rome could seat 250,000 spectators.

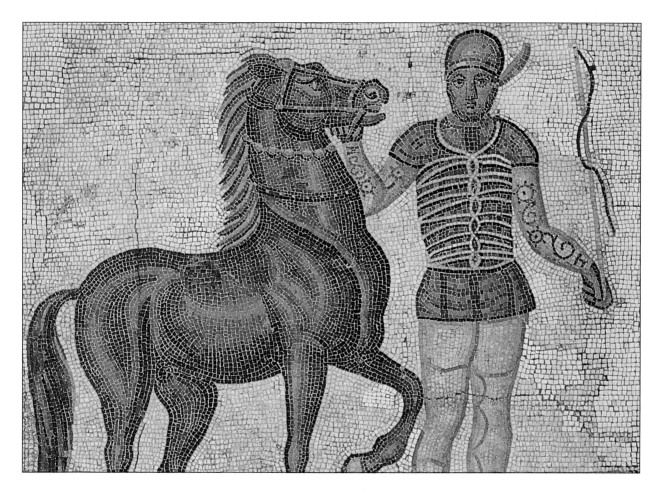

The charioteers were originally of the equestrian class and, although chariots were no longer used for military purposes in the ancient world, driving them remained a socially exclusive activity which could only be demonstrated at religious festivals. Gradually chariot racing lost its religious significance, charioteers became professional performers, but chariot racing remained popular with all social groups. Artistic equestrianism (such as leaping from one horse to another) was also included in the circus entertainment, but never horse racing.

Successful charioteers acquired great fame and wealth, and the names of some of them and their horses still survive on mosaics, glassware and relief sculptures. Chariots were normally drawn by four horses, although two or more could be used. The wooden chariots were lightweight and easily broken. As the races became more varied and dramatic, the most difficult part was at the turning posts where collisions frequently occurred, leading to the deaths of charioteers and horses alike.

Chariot racing was a very expensive and highly organized business run for profit by private enterprises. In Rome there were four racing factions distinguished by their colours – the reds, whites, blues and greens. The charioteers wore the colours of their stables and the greens and blues became the favourites at Rome. There was much rivalry in cities between the different factions and their supporters, which led to frequent outbursts of violence.

END OF THE GAMES

During the 4th century, restrictions were put on the games and they were eventually banned. By the end of the century, the imperial gladiatorial schools had closed down and gladiatorial combats ceased at this time in the Eastern Empire and in the 5th century in the west. Combats with animals seem to have continued in both parts of the empire until the 6th century but public athletics, including the Olympic Games, were banned. Chariot racing disappeared in the West, but it continued in the East for another 1,000 years throughout the Byzantine Empire and into the Middle Ages.

CHAPTER SEVEN

COMMERCE
and
CRAFT

*"At Rome, all things can be had
at a price."*
(JUVENAL, *SATIRES*, iii, 183)

THE PEOPLE AT WORK

Most of the information about the working population in Roman society is derived from representations in art, such as mosaics, wall paintings and sculptured reliefs, particularly those funerary monuments depicting scenes of everyday business life. There are also references in graffiti to various trades, especially the political slogans found on the walls at Pompeii such as 'the barbers want Trebius as *aedile*' (magistrate). Another source of knowledge about crafts and trades within the (magistrate) empire is in the Edict on Maximum Prices published in 301 by Diocletian in an attempt to control prices. The Edict was impossible to enforce, but nevertheless gives useful information on prices, goods and the standard of living. Much information about industry and trade can also be obtained from archaeological excavations, and in particular from the study of finds – both the finished goods and the waste materials.

There are very few references to labourers and craftworkers in the literary sources because they had a low status and did not themselves leave behind written evidence about their everyday lives. There are, however, records of business transactions, usually written on papyri or on waxed, wooden writing tablets. Within the working classes there were divisions between slaves, freedpeople, free citizens and non-citizens, although it is not usually obvious to us which group carried out the different types of work. Most businesses were probably small family-run concerns employing a few slaves and apprentices. In addition to the manufacturers of goods, there were also many traders active throughout the Empire, some of whom were organized in large trading companies or guilds. Traders had a much greater opportunity of acquiring wealth than the craftworkers, and private individuals who had enough capital to make loans could participate in money-lending.

ROMAN JEWELLERY

ABOVE A gold necklace with a pendant made from sheet metal decorated by a Gorgon's head in repoussé work. The pendant is suspended on a gold wire chain and is 3rd century in date.

RIGHT A funerary portrait from Hawara, Egypt. It is painted on wood and shows a woman wearing a necklace and earrings with inset precious stones.

Towns became manufacturing centres, and processed and used the raw materials brought in from the agricultural estates (such as wool, hides, timber, and produce), and from the rural industrial centres (such as stone from the quarries). The most important industry was probably the manufacturing and selling of food and drink, but a vast range of crafts was also carried out.

GOLD

Most mining establishments came under the direct control of the State within the Empire, and gold-mining could be on quite a large scale, as in southern Spain. The gold-bearing ore was extracted from the rock and smelted, and the resulting liquid gold poured into moulds to form ingots. While much of the gold went to the State for official use, such as for coins, some of it was bought by goldsmiths. Their main product was jewellery made from sheet metal, wire, or cast metal. Sheet gold was formed by hammering an ingot on an anvil until it was sufficiently thin. Only a little jewellery was made by casting, as the sheet method used a lot less metal and was therefore cheaper. Wire was normally made by twisting a strip of metal and rolling it between plates of stone or bronze. It was used mainly for ornamental chains and objects such as rings and earrings, also for filigree work. Much gold jewellery was decorated with coloured stone and glass inlays.

SILVER

One of the major silver-producing areas was Spain, where silver was mined along with lead. Silver nearly always occurs in a lead ore called galena, and in order to extract the silver, the lead ore was heated to around 1,000°C (1,800°F), a process known as cupellation. Very little silver jewellery was made, the main products being coins and silver plate. Silversmiths produced quantities of eating and drinking vessels for prosperous households, but silver plate was also made for religious purposes, especially for use by the Christian Church in the later Roman period.

Silver could be hammered into shape and yet it was possible to remove all traces of hammering by careful polishing, so few signs of the manufacturing methods can be seen on Roman objects. Few craftworker's tools have been found, but the techniques were probably similar to those used today. One of the main methods of producing decoration was by the repoussé ('pushed-out') method, which was done by hammering the back of the silver so that the pattern stood out in relief on the other side. For drinking vessels, it was normal for a smooth inner lining of silver to be fitted, so hiding the identations of the repoussé work. One of the finest techniques in silverwork was its combination with glass to produce decorative vessels.

LEAD, TIN AND PEWTER

After silver was extracted from the lead ore at the mines, the lead was cast in moulds to produce large ingots (known as 'pigs'). They weighed around 86 kg (190lb), and often bore the name of the emperor and the centre of production. Lead was used extensively in the building trade for water pipes, bath linings, roofing and cisterns. It was also used for coffins, containers for cremated remains, and smaller objects such as weights and plumb-bobs.

Tin was mined for use as an alloy with other metals, and by the late 3rd century, pewter, an alloy of lead and tin, was used for the production of objects such as plates, dishes and jugs and also used as a solder. Pewter was always cast and several stone moulds have been found. These moulds consisted of two pieces, one of which fitted inside the other leaving a small gap into which the molten metal was poured.

BRONZE

Copper was rarely used on its own but was combined with other metals to form bronze. An alloy of copper and tin was suitable for working when cold to produce small, simple objects, but the most common method of manufacturing bronze objects was by casting, when lead was added to the copper instead. The *cire perdue* ('lost wax') method of casting involved making a model of the object in wax which was then coated with clay or sand with clay. This was heated so that the wax melted and ran out, leaving a hollow into which the molten bronze was poured. The outer clay covering was then broken, leaving a solid cast bronze object. For larger objects such as statues, this method was too expensive, and so the 'hollow cast' method was used. A clay model was made which was coated with a layer of wax on which all the details were sculptured. The wax was in turn coated with

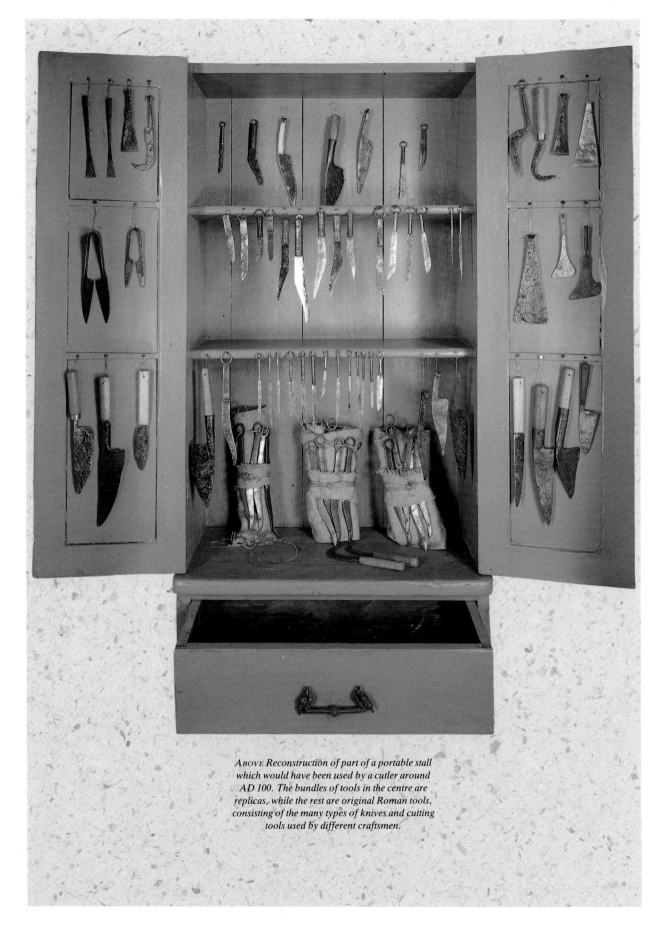

*ABOVE Reconstruction of part of a portable stall
which would have been used by a cutler around
AD 100. The bundles of tools in the centre are
replicas, while the rest are original Roman tools,
consisting of the many types of knives and cutting
tools used by different craftsmen.*

clay, and molten bronze was poured through holes so that it replaced the wax layer, which melted away. The removal of the outer clay layer left a hollow bronze object with a solid core of clay (which was often removed). Very large objects were made in several pieces which were welded together, and some objects, including metal vessels, could be cast in reusable stone moulds.

Thousands of bronzesmiths must have been employed in workshops in the Roman period as a wide range of objects was made in bronze such as coins, pins, needles, toilet instruments, jewellery, lamp holders and tableware, as well as many items of military equipment.

Objects such as plates, brooches and armour were often tinned to make them appear to be silver by pouring molten tin over the surface. A common method of decorating small bronze objects was by enamelling, a process particularly used in the 1st–3rd centuries. Different coloured vitreous (glass) substances were placed in the separate compartments of the piece to be decorated, such as a brooch, and these melted and fused to the bronze when heated. This technique is known as champlevé, and brightly coloured objects were produced in bronze.

IRON

Iron ore was mined extensively using open-cast methods, although some mine shafts are known. The ore was 'roasted' in an open hearth and then melted in a smelting furnace constructed of clay. The molten iron was formed into ingots which could be used by blacksmiths in towns, villas and the army. The blacksmiths heated the iron in a hearth until it was red hot, and then carried it by tongs to the anvil where it was hammered into rough shape. As it cooled, the iron was reheated, and the process was repeated until the required object was formed.

The tools used by the blacksmith were very similar to those of today. Iron was widely used for everyday tools and fittings such as axes, hammers, saws, picks, horseshoes, locks and keys, hinges and nails. It was also used for military equipment including helmets, swords and daggers.

STONE

Stone was rarely used in building in many pre-Roman communities, but its use gradually

LEFT A pair of corroded iron tweezers found in London. Implements such as these tweezers are very similar to ones used today.

increased in towns, forts and villas, and for roads. It was one of the heaviest commodities to be transported in the Roman world and so it was quarried as near as possible to where it was to be used, and then generally transported by water. The techniques of quarrying stone remained unaltered right up to the 20th century, and the quarries were mostly open cast, although some mining for rarer stones took place. Most quarries produced the blocks for

RIGHT Bricks and tiles were made from clay and were then fired in kilns. Here Roman roofing tiles have remained in place from the final firing of the kiln and were never retrieved.

subsequent shaping and carving, but some stoneworking did take place there, such as the roughing out of columns and coffins. Lime production for mortar was often associated with quarrying as lime was obtained by burning limestone in large kilns.

Stone was transported to the workshops for the production of a wide range of objects such as quernstones, tombstones, altars and statues. Softer materials like jet and shale were worked into finer objects such as beads, hairpins, finger-rings, and even table legs. As well as finished objects, some stone was widely traded, particularly precious and semi-precious stones for use in jewellery, and marble and other fine stones for the decoration of buildings.

WOOD

Wood was extensively used in the construction trade, in buildings and as scaffolding. Quantities of timber were also needed for ship building, wharves, and carts. Many everyday objects were also made of wood, including bowls, buckets, barrels, chests, and writing tablets. The timbers were cut initially with large saws operated by two men. Woodworking tools were very similar to those of today, including planes and chisels, and the lathe was widely used in furniture making. Very little Roman wood has survived to the present day, except where it is preserved by special conditions, such as in waterlogged deposits.

BRICK AND TILE

A revolution in Roman construction methods was the use of baked clay bricks and tiles, which are found in vast quantities on excavations of many Roman sites, particularly in areas where suitable local building stone was unavailable. Brick and tile manufacturing was organized on a large scale, by towns and by the army, while there were also numerous smaller tileries and brickworks, some operated on a seasonal basis. The natural clay was dug out and allowed to weather over the winter, after which it was prepared for use. Bricks and tiles were made by placing the clay into moulds and left until it was dry and hard, then they were stacked in a kiln and fired. A variety of sizes of bricks was made,

ABOVE Bricks were often used in walls and arches. In this bath-house (viewed from the exterior) they give a pleasing and decorative effect.

LOCAL POTTERY

ROMAN KILN, SHEPTON MALLET.

LEFT Most pottery consisted of simple earthenware vessels. They were made on a potter's wheel, placed on supports over a furnace in the kiln and then fired. It was normal for pottery to be supplied to fairly local markets as it was a bulky and fragile commodity to transport over long distances.

*Above Samian pottery was glossy fine red
tableware which was made in vast quantities in the
1st and 2nd centuries and was traded all over
the empire.*

as well as a large range of tiles; some were marked using a finger or an official stamp, while others displayed accidental marks such as the pawprints of dogs and cats that ran across them as they were laid out to dry.

Bricks were used for walls and arches and tiles mostly for roofing. Two main types of roof tile were used – a flat tile with flanges (*tegula*) and a curved one (*imbrex*) to cover the gaps between adjoining flat tiles. Tiles were also incorporated into underfloor heating systems (hypocausts) where the floors were supported on pillars of tile (*pilae*) or stone; channels in the walls to conduct gases and hot air used specially made hollow flue tiles.

POTTERY

Pottery vessels for domestic use (especially for the preparation and storage of food) had been made long before the Romans, but with increased demand large potteries grew up in areas with good quality clay. Most pottery consisted of fairly simple earthenware vessels, white, cream, orange, grey or black in colour, usually made on a potter's wheel and then fired in a kiln. This type of pottery (known as 'coarse pottery' or 'kitchen wares') was not traded over wide areas, but supplied local markets. Many shops selling pottery have been found, such as at Pompeii where shops with their contents were engulfed by the volcanic eruption of Vesuvius in 79.

Some pottery was traded over long distances, including the very large vessels known as *amphorae*. These were used as containers for wine, olive oil and fish sauce, which were traded. (Food could also be transported in barrels or sacks, but these have left virtually no trace.) Fine tablewares were popular and therefore traded widely, the most well-known type being samian ware (also known as *terra sigillata*). This was a red glossy surfaced

BELOW A mosaic, made from thousands of tesserae, from Hadrian's Villa at Tivoli near Rome. It depicts a finely worked bowl on which there are four drinking doves, and is a copy of a Greek original by Sosus.

ABOVE The technique of making decorative floors from pieces of marble is known as opus sectile. *This 4th-century work from the basilica of Junius Basso in Rome depicts a tiger seizing a calf.*

pottery first made in northern Italy and subsequently in Gaul and Germany. The earlier pottery was generally plain, but moulds were later used to produce vessels with decoration in relief. The samian pottery industry was organized on a massive scale, and it is found right across the empire, but from the late 2nd century the market for it declined and the North African potteries took over the production of red ware pottery.

INTER OR DECORATION

Most houses had mortar or wooden floors and plain plastered walls, but for those who could afford it interior decoration was an important aspect of life. The finest decorations were reserved for the dining and reception rooms. Skilled workers were responsible for the many mosaic floors, some fairly plain and others with elaborate scenes. The floors had to have solid foundations to prevent cracking and subsidence, and some super-imposed floors have been found where new floors were laid directly on old ones. Mosaic floors were made from small cubes known as *tesserae*, normally of stone, but with some tile, pottery, glass and other materials being used. Errors are visible on some mosaics, while others show signs of repairs. Decorative floors could also be constructed from shaped pieces of coloured marble, a technique known as *opus sectile*.

Mosaics were also used to decorate walls and, unlike floor mosaics, which had a functional purpose and had to be robust, wall mosaics were constructed of more exotic materials, in particular glass *tesserae*. However, walls were usually decorated by paintings, and the plasterer had to produce a very smooth surface on which the designs could be painted. Various pigments, generally made from natural substances, were used for the colours, and it was customary to decorate ceilings in the same way.

TEXTILES

In western Europe sheep were the major source of textile fibres and the wool was shorn with iron shears. Wool was spun with

ABOVE A reconstruction of a dining-room decorated by wall paintings and with various pieces of Roman furniture and other objects. Most wealthy Romans reclined on a couch to eat meals.

LEFT Clothing is commonly portrayed in art forms such as in this statue of a god who is wearing a toga.

hand spindles (not with spinning wheels), and then the fibres were dyed using a variety of pigments. Weaving of the woollen thread was done mainly on vertical, warp-weighted, wooden looms, none of which have survived, although they are represented in art. The woven cloth was subsequently treated by the fuller to remove grease and dirt. This was done by soaking the cloth in tanks of water mixed with 'fuller's earth' or decayed urine (which was collected in large jars provided by the fullers at street corners for the use of passers-by).

Flax was grown for linen and in the Roman period some very fine textiles were produced, including some interwoven with gold thread. Textiles were also transported over vast distances, including silk fabrics and yarn from China. A few textile fragments have survived in waterlogged conditions or as imprints on corroded metal, and clothing is often shown on mosaics and tombstones. The toga was the traditional form of dress for the upper class Roman male and consisted of a single

ROMAN SHOEMAKERS

ABOVE On the left a shoemaker sits on a stool making leather shoes, and he himself wears leather sandals. On top of his cupboard are two pairs of completed shoes. On the right another craftsman is manufacturing rope. This relief sculpture is on a stone sarcophagus.

RIGHT Leather shoes with a decorative openwork design, originally fastened by laces. Even such decorative shoes would usually have had clumsy hob-nailed soles.

long piece of material carefully draped around the body. This form of dress came to be worn less frequently, and was mostly reserved for special occasions. The more common form of dress in the Roman world was the tunic, usually with sleeves, which was secured by brooches (*fibulae*) and by a girdle or belt at the waist. Tunics were worn to just below the knee, although women wore longer ones. Depending on the climate, a cloak and hooded cape was worn as an outer garment, held in place by brooches. Although the styles of clothing were fairly conservative, there was a wide range of fine to coarse materials in various colours. There is also some evidence of knitted socks or stockings worn by women, but otherwise no evidence of leg coverings except boots. Some people may have worn trousers, a north European form of dress which both Greeks and Romans held in contempt as fit only for Barbarians.

Another major product from agricultural estates was hides that were processed into leather by tanning, from which a variety of products could be made such as shoes, clothing, tents, saddles and harness. Some shoes or sandals had heavy clumsy soles with hobnails, usually for military use, but there was more elegant footwear.

GLASS

The invention of glassblowing had an enormous impact on the glass industry because it enabled vessels to be produced much more rapidly and cheaply. Bluish-green glass (a colour produced by the impure raw materials) was most commonly used, but different colours and colourless glass could be achieved by the addition of various ingredients. Glass was used to manufacture vessels either by free blowing, or by blowing into a mould to produce the required shape. Window glass was made by casting in flat moulds or by blowing a cylindrical shape which was cut open and rolled out flat. Although there were other items made of glass, such as bangles and beads, the main production was of glass vessels, ranging from ones with a utilitarian domestic function to some exquisite masterpieces of art, as yet unsurpassed in technical quality and artistry.

DAILY TASKS

The preparation of corn for flour was one of the most important trades, as bread was the staple item of the diet; at Pompeii actual carbonized loaves have been found. Heavy but portable rotary hand mills or querns were used, consisting of two stones with curved grinding surfaces between which the corn was ground. Corn could also be ground in larger types of rotary mills turned by slaves, or by blindfolded donkeys or horses.

Water power was used to a limited extent in the Roman world for pumping excess water out of mines and providing the power to watermills. At Barbegal in France, a large-scale 4th-century flour mill with 16 watermills arranged in a double row has been excavated. The waterwheels were over 7 ft (2 m) in diameter and the water power was provided by water from an aqueduct which descended down the waterwheels at an angle of 30°. It has been calculated that the mills could grind up to 8.8 tons (9 tonnes) of flour every 24 hours, enough to feed the inhabitants of the nearby town of Arles and surrounding district.

The concentration of watermills at Barbegal is unique in the Roman world and generally such large-scale industry and technical innovation were rare. This lack of development was probably due to the effects of slave labour and the plentiful supply of cheap labour in the cities. Roman society never fully developed an industrial economy in the modern sense, but pursued many industries on the level of crafts, which nevertheless reached technical and artistic heights.

BELOW Many fine vessels of glass were made in the Roman period. These three vessels (a cup with both handles broken off and bad irridescent weathering over all its surface, a long-necked flask, and a bowl with a wide flat rim and decorative handle) were all made in transparent colourless glass.

CHAPTER EIGHT

HIGHWAYS *and* BYWAYS

'All roads lead to Rome'
(ANONYMOUS, 14TH-CENTURY PROVERB)

ROAD MAPS

The Romans were frequent travellers and undertook journeys both for military and business purposes, and for pleasure. The long-distance network of communications and transport across the vast Empire was unparalleled until modern times. To assist the traveller, numerous maps and itineraries seem to have been available, and copies of a few have survived. The *Peutinger Table* is a 13th-century copy of a late Roman map of the whole Roman Empire and beyond, from Britain to India, and survives virtually intact. It is a continuous elongated chart 22 ft (6.75 m) long and 13 in (34 cm) wide, and was a road map intended for the imperial courier service (*cursus publicus*). The map is actually a schematic diagram showing the main roads, towns, road stations, rivers, mountains and distances. In all, 555 cities are shown, each represented by small illustrations. The imperial courier service used the main roads which had official stations along them for a change of horse and an overnight halt. For the ordinary traveller there were staging posts or inns (mansiones) where the distance between two towns was too great to travel in one day.

The *Antonine Itinerary* was a 3rd-century compilation of routes all over the empire and included lists of the *mansiones* with the distances between them. Many of the roads and places have been identified. Another useful document to have survived is the *Ravenna Cosmography* which gives place-names, river names and landscape details. It was compiled by a monk in the Middle Ages from a series of much earlier documents. Roman literary accounts give some information on travel, and Diocletian's Edict on Prices, which included transport, has enabled direct comparisons of costs to be made between the Roman Empire, the Medieval period and the modern world.

ROAD CONSTRUCTION

There were roads in many places before the Romans, but these were largely local and long-distance trackways which followed the topography of the region. Roman roads were

BELOW Masonry road bridges of the Roman period survive throughout the Empire. This one at Vaison-la-Romaine in southern France is still used for road traffic. It was built of huge blocks of masonry held together without any mortar. Only the parapet has been replaced, having been washed away in floods in 1616. The bridge even survived a direct hit by a German bomb in 1944.

LEFT A Roman road with a paved surface running over the moor at Blackstone Edge in Greater Manchester. The central rut is thought to have been deliberately cut to hold the brake-poles of the carts.

deliberately planned and constructed, and the major routes were built initially by the army for strategic reasons. Other main roads were also constructed at State expense, although the cost of maintenance usually fell on the local community. From the main roads led a series of local roads which were financed by the local town councils, and there were also private roads across estates, built and maintained by the landowners. The number and total length of local roads must have far exceeded the major roads, although the major roads are the ones that usually survive today.

Roman roads are renowned for their straightness, but they often took detours rather than traverse difficult terrain. However, the engineers were quite capable of designing roads to cross ground such as marshland whenever necessary. The roads were laid out by surveyors and then constructed by digging down to a firm foundation which was reinforced by ramming brushwood or by driving in wooden piles. Layers of stones, sand and gravel were deposited on the foundation, and were sometimes built up as an embankment (known as an *agger*) to assist drainage, with side drainage ditches as well. The manner in which roads were constructed depended on the firmness of the subsoil and on the available materials. The final road surface often consisted of substantial paving stones held in place by a kerb on either side of the road, or otherwise crushed stones or gravel were used. Many roads display signs of subsequent repair and resurfacing.

Caravan roads in the desert have left little evidence on the ground apart from rows of small rocks and stones which were pushed to each side to make the routes easier for the pack animals. The routes can also be plotted from the existence of posting stations, wells and water tanks built by the Romans, some of which are still in use today.

Along the roads just outside the towns were the cemeteries, and funerary monuments lined the routes for all travellers to see. (It was illegal to bury the dead inside towns.) Inside old cities such as Rome, the street system was irregular, but in new towns it was carefully planned. The streets were often paved, as at Pompeii where stepping stones were provided for pedestrians. The ruts left by waggons in the streets and in the country roads indicate the great volume of traffic, although some ruts were deliberately cut to guide vehicles.

BRIDGES

Rivers could be crossed by fords, some of which were paved with stone, and ferries were also used. Many bridges were constructed of timber and were of varying complexity, some being built on piles with iron-clad tips. Timber bridges rarely survive, but they are shown in relief sculptures. Some bridges were built entirely of stone, and in the Mediterranean regions they could be constructed by erecting the piers directly on the river bed when it was dry in the summer. In temperate Europe, the piers had to be constructed with the aid of piles and timber scaffolding which was a more complex process. There were several masonry bridges in Rome, some of which survive today, while across the Empire there is evidence of many others. Some bridges were embellished by triumphal arches, and also had inscriptions and milestones.

MILESTONES

The Roman mile was a thousand Roman paces (1,611 yds or 1,472.5 m). Thus milestones were erected every thousand Roman paces, although in Gaul the league (2,430 yds/2221.2 m) was used as the unit of measurement. Milestones were typically cylindrical or oval-sectioned columns of stone, set on a square base, and were usually 5½–13 ft (2–4 m) in height and 20–30 in (50–80 cm) in diameter. Some had carved inscriptions giving the name of the builder or restorer of the road and distances to the nearest towns, while others had painted directions, long since worn away.

The famous 'golden milestone' was erected in Rome in 20 BC by Augustus, and consisted of a marble column to which were attached gilt-bronze plates displaying the distances from the major towns in the empire.

Over 4,000 milestones have been recorded with Latin inscriptions, and a similar number in Greek. Some milestones are still in place, but most have been re-used, sometimes as road ballast or as columns in churches. Apart from giving distances, the milestones also acted as boundary markers for farming estates and from the documentary evidence many continued to serve this purpose in the Medieval period.

ROAD TRANSPORT

People travelled a great deal on foot, even for long distances, and the horse, mule and donkey were used as pack animals. Some people travelled on horseback, though, and various pieces of horse harness such as snaffle and curb-bits have been discovered in excavations. Iron horseshoes have been found, but not stirrups as these were not used.

Our knowledge of vehicles is fairly limited, mainly based on sculptures and literary evidence. Carts and chariots were well developed in the pre-Roman Celtic world, and many types of similar wheeled vehicles must have been used by the Romans. These probably ranged from large solid-wheeled carts pulled by oxen to light carriages pulled by horses. There is some evidence for the use of suspension in passenger vehicles, which may have made travelling more comfortable, but otherwise the most comfortable way to travel was probably in a litter carried by slaves.

The amount of traffic in towns was so great that in Julius Caesar's time the entry of

ABOVE A four-wheeled carriage pulled by two horses, carved on a sarcophagus.

wheeled vehicles into Rome was restricted, and these restrictions were later extended to other parts of the Empire. Wheeled vehicles were then only allowed through the city streets at night, an early example of the control of urban traffic congestion.

WATER TRANSPORT

Despite the fine roads, transport by road could still be very expensive, especially for bulky goods, and so water transport was most important. There were miles of navigable rivers, some of which had been improved by the construction of canals, and numerous flat-bottomed barges were used on them. Rafts and other boats of simple construction were also used, especially in places like Egypt, and pre-Roman techniques of boat building persisted.

In the early Republic there was hardly any tradition of seafaring, but this situation soon changed as it was quicker to travel long distances and more convenient to transport heavy goods by sea. Merchant ships became

WATER TRANSPORT

ABOVE A reconstruction by Ronald Embleton of a water-front scene at the port of London at low tide. Small boats and clinker-built craft with hulls sheathed in lead are moored. Pedestrians and people on horseback are travelling across the wooden bridge over the River Thames.

RIGHT Native traditions of boat building persisted in many parts of the Roman world. This mosaic from Pompeii shows a scene from the River Nile with a native boat being used as a ferry.

LEFT This was one of two lighthouses which guarded the entrance to the harbour at Dover, England.

ABOVE Amphorae were large pottery vessels used for transporting commodities such as wine, olive oil and fish sauce.

clay tiles. The ships were steered by long oars at the stern and several anchors were usually provided, particularly on the bigger ships. Anchors were of wood with lead fittings, but from the 2nd century they began to be replaced by anchors with iron fittings. Hundreds of lead stocks up to a ton in weight have been found in the Mediterranean.

CARGOES

In excavations of shipwrecks, many objects of everyday use have been found, including tableware, quernstones, and terracotta oil lamps. Most Roman merchant ships were small, carrying on average 150 tons (152.5 tonnes), but loads up to 300 tons (304.7 tonnes) could be transported. Cargoes were usually mixed, but a major commodity was wine carried in large amphorae. They were also used to carry other goods such as grain, olive oil and fish sauce (*garum*). Many amphorae have stamps on their handles, usually of the manufacturer or place of origin, especially if they contained wine, and some and some have traces of painted inscriptions giving details of the shippers, contents and date. Another clue to the date of the cargo is the style of the amphora itself which changed throughout the Roman period.

Some of the shipwrecks in the Mediterranean could carry at least 5,000 amphorae at a time. They were stacked in layers with the points of the upper layers of amphorae fitted between the necks of those below. The extensive sea trade is vividly represented by the Monte Testaccio in Rome, close to the River Tiber. It is an immense dump of amphorae fragments which is 115 ft (42 m) high and 930 yds (1,017 m) round.

HARBOURS

It was possible for small vessels to unload their cargoes on beaches but larger ships required harbours for docking and shelter from the weather. The remains of Roman harbours with monumental quays and docking areas survive all around the Mediterranean, and these involved engineering and construction work on a large scale. There were also riverside wharves in places like Rome and London, with timber-revetted waterfronts and huge warehouses. Lighthouses were an important addition to harbour entrances, and by 400 over 30 lighthouses are known to have existed in the Roman world.

so big that barges had to take goods from the ships up the River Tiber to Rome, leading to the growth of Ostia at the mouth of the river as a very important and busy port.

There is evidence for the appearance of ships in ancient literature and in representations in art (although quite often of a schematic nature and not accurate). This information is being supplemented by underwater excavations of Roman wrecks, and over 500 shipwrecks of this period are known in the Mediterranean. Wrecks of seafaring ships of the Roman period are virtually unknown outside the Mediterranean, although river craft have been found.

The most notable feature of Roman ships was a rigid outer shell built first, in contrast to later ships when the frame was constructed first. In the Mediterranean region, the planks of the shell were fitted edge-to-edge (carvel-built) and held in place by wooden pegs (treenails) or long copper nails, while north European ships were mainly constructed from overlapping planks secured by iron nails (clinker-built). The hulls of the Mediterranean ships were mostly of pine, cypress or cedar, with frames of oak; the lower part of the hull was often sheathed in lead as a defence against wood-boring sea worms. The north European ships were constructed mainly of oak.

When the shell of the ship was complete, the internal frames, strengthening timbers, decks and masts were added. There was a large mast amidships to carry a rectangular mainsail, and sometimes small masts near the stern and bow. Evidence has been found on the galley roof being covered in baked

CHAPTER NINE

RITUAL
and
RELIGION

"And how can man die better,
Than facing fearful odds,
For the ashes of his fathers,
And the temples of his Gods."
(LORD MACAULAY *HORATIUS*, VERSE 27)

GODS AND SOCIETY

Religion was an essential part of Roman society, and nearly every activity was governed by deities, some of which were gods and others merely vaguely defined spirits. Roman religion had many different gods, and during the Republic more gods were assimilated from the Etruscans, and later from the Greeks. Rather than simply adopt new gods, their functions were identified and combined with those of the existing Roman gods.

The main Olympian gods (so-called because they were identified with the Greek gods who lived on Mount Olympus in Greece) were Jupiter, Juno and Minerva. The Greek god Zeus was compared with the Roman god Jupiter, and became father and king of the gods, also responsible for the weather, especially storms. Juno, who became his wife and queen of the gods, was the goddess of marriage and women, and was identified with the Greek goddess Hera. Minerva (equivalent to the Greek goddess Athena) was the goddess of war and of wisdom. These three deities were often called the Capitoline triad because of shrines dedicated to them on the Capitoline Hill at Rome.

Other major Olympian deities included Mars (god of war), Mercury (god of trade and messenger of the gods) and Bacchus (god of grapes and wine production). The Greek-style gods soon became part of Rome's religious tradition, and because they were already well-developed mythological figures, it was easy to portray them in art and literature. The Romans continued to import deities, sometimes deliberately as happened in 293 BC when Aesculapius, the Greek god of medicine, was adopted because of a plague at Rome.

The Romans had a vast number of minor deities, and nearly every aspect of life had its own spirit, including personified virtues such as victory and fortune. People only worshipped those deities and spirits most closely associated with their own lives. There were spirits in the fields and woods, and each tree or stream acquired its own spirit, such as the spirit of the River Tiber. There were also spirits in the home, including Vesta who was the goddess of the hearth fire and the Penates, the spirits of the cupboard or pantry. Each household had its own Lar, a spirit or deity which guarded and protected the household

and its members, and it was the responsibility of the household to maintain a shrine (*larium*) in the home, at which sacrifices were made regularly. The cautious attitude of the Romans to such spirits is exemplified by dedications of altars to the 'gods that inhabit this place', ensuring that no god could be offended by being overlooked, even if they remained unnamed.

In the eastern Mediterranean, people had worshipped their kings as gods for centuries. When conquered by the Romans, they regarded their new rulers as divine figures, but this was discouraged. Instead, they were encouraged to worship 'Roma', the divine spirit of Rome, but when Julius Caesar died, he was made a god, and from then onwards it was normal practice for emperors to be deified and worshipped after their deaths (unless their memory was damned, *damnatio*

ABOVE One of the Olympian deities was Diana, the goddess of fertility and of the hunt, who was always portrayed with arrows.

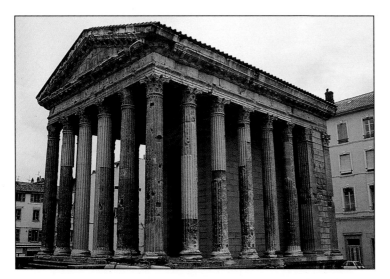

memoriae). The Imperial Cult and the associated worship of 'Roma' became an important element in Roman religion.

STATE OBSERVANCE

The purpose of Roman religion was to gain the goodwill of the divine forces and to keep them benevolent, since that would ensure individual and collective success and prosperity. Early Roman religion developed as part of the rituals of farming when it was essential that the rituals were performed correctly to maintain good relationships with the spirits. Roman religion was not concerned with ethical and moral behaviour, but only with the correct observance of the rituals, which in time became static and mechanical.

The State religion involved the worship of 'Roma', the Imperial Cult and the accepted classical deities, and was very much a public rather than a private religion, with the ceremonies and rituals being performed correctly to ensure the goodwill of the gods – the *pax deorum*. Temples and religious festivities received State funding, and the priests were State officials, for whom being a priest was a mark of social distinction. The emperor was the Pontifex Maximus, the head of the State religion.

The Romans communicated with the gods by sacrifice, prayer, vow and divination. There were fixed days for festivals when they could review their relationships with the various deities, and when prayers and sacrifices usually took place outside the temple of the deity. Especially at State-funded sacrifices, the main victims were cattle, sheep, goats and pigs.

ABOVE This Classical temple at Vienne in France was originally dedicated to the imperial cult – 'Roma' and the deified Augustus – but it was later rededicated to Augustus and his wife Livia. It is one of the Empire's best-preserved temples.

ABOVE RIGHT A relief sculpture on a funerary monument depicting the construction of a Classical-style temple. A crane is being powered by slaves on a treadmill.

On some occasions the support of the god was invoked by means of a vow rather than a prayer or sacrifice, when a gift (votive offering) was promised to the god only if the supplicant's wishes were fulfilled. In order to interpret signs sent by the gods, divination was practised, and this included inspecting the internal organs of a sacrificial animal.

TEMPLES

The style of Roman temples was much influenced by Greek architecture. Many were rectangular in shape, with an elevated podium and a portico or deep-set porch, approached by a flight of steep steps. The side and end columns could be 'engaged', that is, built into the side walls so that only part of their circumference protruded beyond the walls. During the empire, most of the columns were in the Corinthian style with ornately carved capitals.

Apart from the traditional classical design, temples were built to a variety of plans and sizes, including circular and triangular examples, culminating in the Pantheon at Rome which had a huge dome open to the sky at the very top. There were also native-style temples such as the Romano-Celtic temples in northern Europe. These were square or polygonal and surrounded by a portico consisting either of an open colonnade or a solid wall with windows. In addition, there were

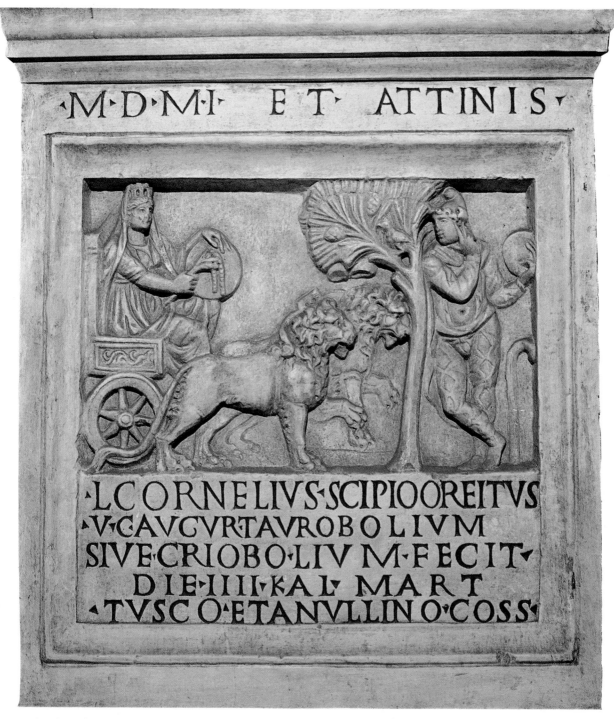

ABOVE An altar to the eastern goddess Cybele. Nearby stands her consort, the god Attis. The inscription refers to taurobolium, a ceremony performed by several eastern cults but which originated with Cybele. The worshipper stood in a pit and was bathed in the blood of a bull sacrificed over him or her.

many simple shrines and temples throughout the Roman world.

The main purpose of a temple was to house the cult figures and to provide an inner sanctum for the priests. The worshippers assembled outside the temple where there was usually a courtyard and the main sacrificial altar. All the public religious ceremonies took place in this area, and the courtyards were frequently surrounded by colonnades as protection against unfavourable weather.

RELIGIOUS TOLERANCE

The Roman authorities were fairly tolerant of the religious practices of the people they conquered, although they suppressed religions that were considered to be against the State, such as the Druids in northern Gaul and Britain and also Judaism and Christianity. The Romans did their best not to offend any deity, even those of their enemies, and so instead of driving out the gods of newly conquered territory, there was often a fusion be-

tween local and classical gods, and the local gods continued to be worshipped as well. This can be seen at Bath in England, for example, where a Classical-style temple was dedicated to Sulis Minerva. The name Sulis is that of a local Celtic nymph who was linked with the Roman goddess Minerva.

THE MYSTERY RELIGIONS
By the late Republic, Romans became acquainted with many eastern religions from places such as Asia Minor, Egypt and beyond. These religions were very different from the Roman State religion and are often called

ABOVE Priests performing religious rites outside a temple dedicated to the eastern goddess Isis. Most religious ceremonies took place in a courtyard outside temples. This ceremony was depicted in a wall-painting at Herculaneum.

'mystery' religions because they involved new converts in mysterious initiation ceremonies. They offered personal salvation to individuals and appealed to all social classes and races. Most Romans did not renounce the State religion once they had been initiated into a new eastern religion, as no conflict was perceived between the two – eastern religions were private and personal while the State religion remained public and impersonal.

The main eastern cults were those of Mithras, Cybele, Isis and Bacchus. The cult of Cybele, 'The Great Mother', was the only one that was deliberately introduced into

MITHRAISM

ABOVE The god Mithras is slaying a bull from whose blood life grows. Mithraism was a popular eastern religion, particularly with the army and merchants as it was an exclusively male cult. The slaying of the bull took place in a cave, and so Mithraic temples were often built underground.

Bacchus was originally one of the Olympian gods (identified with the Greek god Dionysus), but the Bacchanalia (the often drunken celebrations in honour of the god of wine) were restricted in 186 BC by the Senate, as it was thought that the religion was becoming politically subversive. However, the religion was not totally suppressed and emerged again as one of the mystery religions, and Bacchus was even believed by many Romans to have originated from India and not to be one of the Olympian gods (where Dionysus was the twelfth of the gods of Mount Olympus).

CHRISTIANITY

The Roman world was initially tolerant of the new eastern religion of Christianity, and it became well established in Rome by the mid 1st century. However, the rites came to be misunderstood and Christians were regarded as atheists because, unlike other eastern religions, converts were expected to

FAR RIGHT A marble head of the god Serapis, Egyptian god of the underworld. The corn measure on his head is a symbol of fertility, which Serapis represented, and is adorned by an olive tree with leaves and berries. It was buried with a group of other sculptures under the Mithraeum in London in the 4th century, possibly to prevent desecration by the Christians. It was found in 1954 and is 17 in (431 mm) high.

Rome. This happened in 205 BC in response to an oracle which required Rome to welcome the goddess if Hannibal was to be defeated.

The best-known eastern cult was that of Mithras which originated in Persia and spread across the whole Roman Empire. Mithras was a god of light, engaged in a constant struggle with Ariman, the evil prince of darkness. Mithras was often portrayed slaying a bull, symbolic of his role as a creative god, with the blood of the bull being the source of life. Mithraism was an exclusively male cult, and was especially popular in the army and with merchants.

The cult of Isis originated in ancient Egypt and reached Rome in the 1st century BC. It flourished despite being suppressed by Octavian because it was the religion of his enemy Cleopatra. Isis was a mother goddess figure and wife of the Egyptian god Serapis.

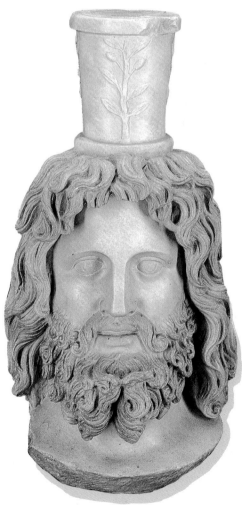

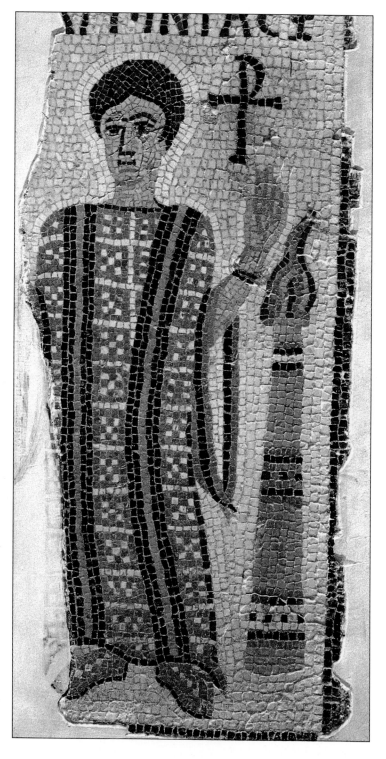

ABOVE An early Christian funerary mosaic of the 4th-5th centuries from Tunisia. The symbol is a Chi-Rho – the first two letters of the Greek word for Christ.

they were no longer required to participate in the rites of the State religion.

Although Christianity began as a religion for the poorer classes, it acquired more and more wealth, and the conversion of the Roman world to this new religion was fairly rapid and extensive. At the end of the 4th century, Theodosius I abolished pagan sacrifice, closed all pagan temples (some of which were destroyed) and confiscated their estates, although the traditional games and festivals continued. Christianity became the official State religion, and followers suppressed the religious freedom of other groups and even persecuted non-Christians. The early Christian Church was from time to time rent by schisms, which caused serious political rifts, but the religion even managed to survive the Barbarian invasions.

Pagan traditions persisted as they were so deeply rooted in Roman society. It was not possible to abolish popular pagan holidays and so, instead, they were combined with Christian festivals. A popular festival in the Roman world was the Lupercalia, on 15 February, which was associated with farming and fertility. In 494 Pope Gelasius I declared that date to be the festival of the Purification of the Virgin Mary, so ensuring its success, and the eve of the festival of the Lupercalia has now become St Valentine's Day. Similarly the Saturnalia was one of the most popular festivals of the whole year, celebrated at the winter solstice. It originally took place for one day on 17 December, but by the late Republic it had extended to several days. This particular festival was not marked by public games, but was a time for family dinners, parties, gift giving, wishing friends and neighbours well, and when masters waited on their slaves. Its place was consequently taken over by Christmas in the Christian calendar, and yet the character of the celebrations has survived to the present day and these elements of ancient paganism have spread around the world.

BURIAL OF THE DEAD

The laws relating to the burial of the dead forbade interment of bodies or their cremated ashes within the boundary of a town or fort, except for children under ten days old (who had no legal existence). Cemeteries are therefore usually found lining the main roads just outside towns, and funerary monuments

renounce all other beliefs. To the Romans this was a crime against the State, and so Christians began to be persecuted for political rather than for religious reasons. The most systematic persecutions took place from the mid to late 3rd century, but in the early 4th century the emperor Constantine was converted to Christianity. He consequently allowed Christians freedom of worship and

LEFT The 6th-century Byzantine basilica at Porec in Yugoslavia with fine Christian wall mosaics.

BELOW A 5th-century mosaic representing an early Christian basilica with two naves and an aisle.

105

SYMMACHORVM

were erected so they could be seen from the roads. The cemetery of Alyscamps at Arles in France was just outside the Roman town on the road to Italy. It was one of the most famous sacred sites of the Roman West, and became a Christian burial ground with thousands of graves growing up around the tomb of St Geneseus.

Most Romans had fairly simple funerals but those of upper-class families could be very elaborate. It was thought that the souls went to the underworld (Hades) after death, rather than to heaven or hell. Sometimes a coin was placed in the mouth of the corpse as the fee to Charon, the ferryman of the river Styx, who carried the person to Hades. The coin was placed in the mouth as both hands would have held cakes for the three heads of the dog Cerberus, guardian of the underworld. Those souls whom the gods of the underworld would not admit were destined to wander for eternity. Consequently, it was thought that a proper burial was essential, and so many Romans belonged to funeral clubs to ensure that this was carried out.

Ashes from cremations were usually placed in containers of pottery, glass or lead which were buried. The position of the burial could be marked by an upright tombstone with a carved inscription about the dead person, and possibly a pictorial representation taken from the person's life or funerary banquet. Some cremations were placed in masonry mausolea (*columbaria*) and a few were covered by mounds of earth.

Inhumations became more popular in the later Empire and usually involved the burial of the dead in a coffin, although for the poor a sack or shroud would have been used. Coffins were of wood, lead or stone, and some bodies were partially embalmed by pouring liquid plaster of Paris around the body. Some stone coffins were extremely ornate and intended for display rather than for burial in the ground.

Grave goods were placed in cremation and inhumation burials, and often included refreshments for the journey to the underworld, shoes for travelling there, and the person's most valued possessions. Some of the coffins and mausolea were robbed in the Roman period, and as the rise of Christianity led to a decline in the use of grave goods, most Roman burials that are excavated are found to have only a few simple grave goods.

FAR LEFT An ivory diptych of the late 4th century portraying a priestess making offerings at a pagan altar. The diptych is headed "SYMMACHORUM" and there is a companion "NICOMACHORUM". Quintus Aurelius Symmachus and Nicomachus Flavianus attempted to revive pagan cults in Rome when Christianity was taking over.

LEFT Pottery vessels were sometimes decorated by schematic faces. These face pots were used as storage jars and for cooking. Some have been found buried as ritual deposits in graves, and others were used to contain cremations. It is possible that the faces were intended to resemble a particular deity.

RIGHT Les Alyscamps ('Elysian Fields') was an immense cemetery just outside Arles on the road to Italy. From the 4th century it became a Christian cemetery and expanded considerably throughout the Middle Ages. Nowadays only the plain sarcophagii have been left in place. The cemetery began to decline in the 15th century and the finest ornate sarcophagi were taken to museums, or given as gifts, and many have been lost. One consignment being loaded in a boat on the River Rhone was so heavy that the boat sank.

CHAPTER TEN

RETREAT
and
RECESSION

'While stands the Coliseum,
Rome shall stand; when falls the
Coliseum, Rome shall fall; and
when Rome falls – the World'
(LORD BYRON, *CHILDE HAROLD'S PILGRIMAGE*,
CANTO IV, CXIV)

ECONOMIC CRISIS

During the first two centuries of the Roman Empire, the provinces became increasingly wealthy, but then the economy of the Empire weakened due to a variety of reasons including a rigid financial policy, the scarcity of slaves and other workers for the agricultural estates, the lack of profitable new territory to annex and exploit, increased taxation, and the immense cost of maintaining the extensive frontiers with a huge army. Matters were made worse when armies returning from the east in 166 introduced plague into the Western Empire, seriously affecting the population.

The Roman coinage was gradually debased, and instead of gold and silver coins being worth the weight of their metal content, they were replaced by a base metal token coinage. A severe shortage of precious metals in the later 3rd century forced the government to issue silver-washed bronze coins. This situation led to progressively higher prices, coins were hoarded and the economic crisis worsened. There was reduced economic activity, new public buildings became much less common, and the cities themselves were neglected. In the first half of the 4th century there was an improvement in the economy, due partly to monetary and taxation reform, but inflation was not brought to a halt.

HOUSE OF CONSTANTINE

Constantine I, the Great, reunited the empire in 324 and reigned as sole Augustus until his death in 337. He was converted to Christianity, which gradually became a unifying force in the Empire. The division in the Empire between east and west still persisted in that two of his sons, Constantius II and Constantine II, served as Caesars. After his death, the Empire was again split between two Augustii; his sons Constantine II and Constans initially ruled the west and Constantius II the east, but Constantine II was eliminated after three years. In 350 Constans fell to a military usurper, Magnentius, but in an ensuing civil war, Constantius II defeated him and so was left in charge of the entire Empire.

Constantine I made Constantinople (now Istanbul) his new capital and the city continued to grow rapidly in splendour and size. In 359 Constantius II gave the city a senate, thereby awarding it constitutional parity with Rome. Meanwhile, the city of Rome was also emerging as an important centre of Christian culture and from the time of Constantine I was embellished by many religious buildings.

In 355 Constantius II appointed his nephew Julian as Caesar in Gaul, mainly to suppress the invading Germanic tribes (Alamanni and

LEFT The head from a giant bronze statue of Constantine I.

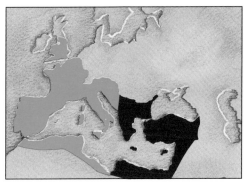

LEFT The division of the Roman world into eastern and western empires.

FAR LEFT Constans was Emperor of the Western Empire after the death of his father Constantine I in 337, but fell to the usurper Magnentius in 350.

Franks) who had crossed the Rhine. Two years later Julian succeeded in forcing them back across the Rhine and in 361 he rebelled against Constantius II, but the latter died of natural causes before a conflict broke out. Julian was killed two years later during a campaign against Persia, bringing the dynasty of Constantine to an end.

BARBARIAN INVASIONS

On his death, Julian's successor was Jovian, who was proclaimed by the army in Mesopotamia, but he died a few months later. Valentinian I (364–375) was then brought to power by the army as emperor of the Western Empire, while his brother Valens was chosen to rule the Eastern Empire. In 367 there was

a major Barbarian invasion of Britain, but this was suppressed within two years by Valentinian's general Count Theodosius, who restored and reinforced the line of forts along Britain's northern frontier and along the coast. The reign of Valentinian I was also devoted to improving the defence of the frontiers of the Rhine and Danube.

When Valentinian I died of apoplexy in 375 he was succeeded in the west by his sons Gratian and Valentinian II, both of whom were controlled by advisers, while Valens remained emperor in the east. At this time there were large-scale movements of Germanic peoples (Barbarians to the Romans), such as the Visigoths, Ostrogoths, Alans, Alemanni, Franks, Burgundians, Vandals, and Suebi. The Huns pushed forward from even further afield, and in turn caused hundreds of thousands of dispossessed Goths (Ostrogoths and Visigoths) and Alans to flee southwards to the Danube. Valens gave permission for thousands of Visigoths to cross into the empire in 376 in order to strengthen his frontier zone and to provide new recruits for the army. However, the settlement was totally mismanaged by the Romans, and in the resulting chaos the Ostrogoths joined the Visigoths. Valens therefore marched against the Goths in 378, but on 9 August the Roman army was defeated at the Battle of Adrianople (now Edirne in European Turkey), and Valens was killed.

RIGHT Valentinian I (364–375) spent much of his reign consolidating the defences of the frontiers which had been weakened by various incursions, particularly along the Rhine and Danube.

LEFT Pevensey fort was shown in the Notitia Dignitatum as Anderidos. The fort was positioned on the coast as a defence against Germanic invasion.

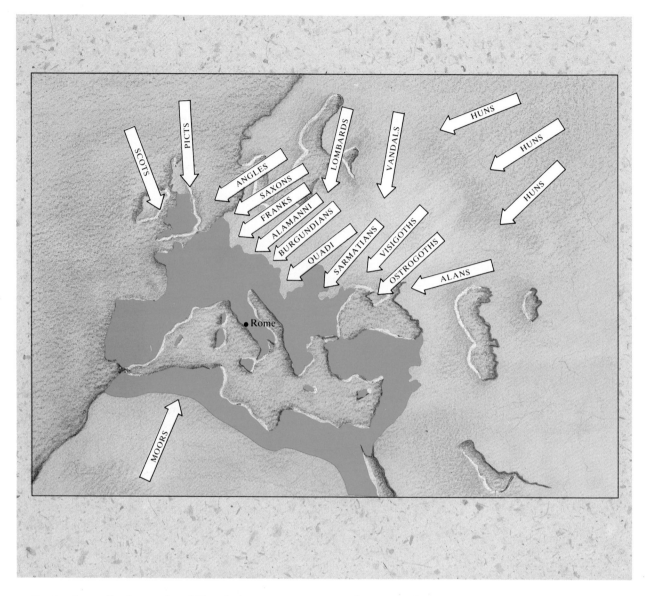

ABOVE The movement of invading tribes into the Roman Empire.

Gratian immediately appointed Theodosius (a Spanish general and the son of Valentinian's former general) to take charge in the East. Theodosius I (379–395) gradually restored order and the Ostrogoths were forced back beyond the frontier. The Visigoths were allowed to settle in the Danube provinces and to serve in the Roman army as *federates* under their own tribal leaders.

In 383 Gratian was murdered at Lyon in an army revolt led by the British usurper Magnus Maximus, who set up his court at Trier. Four years later, after he had campaigned in Gaul and Spain and restored order there, Maximus invaded Italy and deposed Valentinian II. The following year he was defeated and killed by Theodosius I, and Valentinian II was restored to power, but was found dead in 392 (possibly as a result of suicide). Theodosius I therefore took over the rule of the entire Empire. The Visigoths had helped Theodosius in his campaign against the usurper Maximus, but they then refused to return home, and wandered through Macedonia pillaging the province.

When Theodosius I died in 395, he was succeeded by his sons, 18-year-old Arcadius in the east and ten-year-old Honorius in the west. The latter was dominated by the commander Stilicho who remained in virtual control of the west for the next 13 years. Stilicho was the son of a Vandal leader who had joined the Romans and become commander-in-chief under Theodosius.

In the same year the Visigoths, under their newly elected leader Alaric, invaded Greece, and then in 401 made their way to Italy in search of new homelands, and besieged Milan. While the Western Empire began to disintegrate, the eastern empire prospered, enabling the Byzantine Empire to develop its own rich culture. In 402 Stilicho managed to beat back the Visigoths with the aid of the Alans and Vandals, who he then allowed to cross from the province of Pannonia into Noricum in return for their services.

Stilicho subsequently arranged to make use of Alaric and the Visigoths to secure control of Illyricum (modern-day Yugoslavia and Albania) over whose territory he was in dispute with Constantinople. However, he was prevented from doing this by major Barbarian invasions in Gaul and a usurpation in Britain. Alaric nevertheless demanded payment for his unused services, but this was refused, and so he invaded Italy again in 408. Stilicho was executed on the emperor's orders for alleged complicity with Alaric, and in the same year the emperor Arcadius died and was succeeded by his son Theodosius II. Alaric went on to besiege Rome, which he captured and sacked in 410.

St Jerome wrote from Bethlehem: 'When the brightest light of the whole earth was extinguished, when the Roman Empire was deprived of its head, when the whole world perished in one city, then I was dumb with silence, I held my peace even from God, and my sorrow was stirred'.

THE COLLAPSE OF THE WESTERN EMPIRE

The fall of Rome had relatively little military significance, since the emperor and government had moved to the safety of Ravenna in northern Italy, in 402, following the siege of Milan. Ravenna became the capital city and a major centre of Christian culture for more than three centuries. The Visigoths continued moving southwards into Italy intending to proceed to Africa, but Alaric died and instead they returned northwards. In Rome there was an economic recovery, with a literary and cultural revival, and the 5th century became a time of building great monumental churches in the city.

In 412 the Visigoths seized part of south-western Gaul, but they were then forced into Spain. Eventually, in 418, they reached agreement with the Roman government to settle in Aquitaine, and from time to time they fought as *federates* on the side of Rome against other invaders.

Far worse than the sack of Rome by Alaric

LEFT Arcadius (395–408) was Emperor of the eastern Empire, succeeding his father Theodosius I. His brother Honorius became Emperor of the western Empire.

was the winter of 406–7, when the Rhine frontier was overrun. Hordes of Germanic peoples, mainly Vandals, Suebi, Burgundians and Alans crossed the frozen Rhine and captured cities in Gaul. There was consternation in Britain, and so the usurper Constantine III crossed from Britain to Gaul in 407 to deal with the worsening military situation. He established his court at Arles, and created a new Gallic empire, restoring order in Britain, Gaul, Germany and Spain. In the winter of 409, the Vandals, Suebi and Alans forced their way across the Pyrenees to Spain, and Constantine III's temporary Empire fell apart. Britain was never recovered, and the year 410 is usually regarded as the end of Roman Britain. Roman civilization tended to die out in northern Gaul and Germany from this time, and in the following year Constantine III was defeated by the imperial army from Ravenna and executed.

The Vandals subsequently joined forces with the Alans, whose king assumed the title 'Rex Vandalorum et Alanorum'. In 429, led by Gaiseric, they crossed the Straits of Gibraltar into Africa. Much of North Africa then fell to the Vandals, and by 439 they had marched eastwards and taken Carthage.

In a brief period of some fifty years from 375 when the Visigoths first appeared on the Danube, the great migratory movements of the various tribes caused the disintegration of the Western Empire. The emperor Honorius, who died in 423, was succeeded by the usurper Johannes for two years, and then four-year-old Valentinian III (425–455) was installed. For a while the general Flavius Aëtius maintained Roman rule in Gaul and undertook several successful campaigns in the

ABOVE From the 6th century, after the Byzantine reconquest of Italy, Rome and other towns were neglected. Monuments and buildings disintegrated and became at least partly buried by a build-up of dirt and debris. This 18th-century etching by GB Piranesi shows the appearance of the ruins of the forum at Rome at that time.

430s and 440s. Meanwhile the Huns, under Attila, were building up strength but were defeated in 451 by a combined force of Romans, Visigoths, Franks and Burgundians near Châlon-sur-Marne. Attila retreated from Gaul and began to plunder Italy, but was persuaded to withdraw. When he died in 453, the Empire of the Huns fell apart. Aëtius was assassinated the following year at the instigation of Valentinian III, who was himself assassinated in 455. This marked the end of the dynasty of Theodosius and was followed by several short-lived emperors.

By this time, the Visigoths had penetrated into Spain, annexing most of the peninsula. The Vandals under Gaiseric advanced from Africa and in 455 spent a fortnight sacking Rome. They then left Italy, acquiring Sicily on the way. By 475 little of the Western Empire remained, although emperors of a kind continued to be nominated. Romulus Augustulus was deposed in 476, and is regarded as the last Roman emperor in the west. Rome as a state had ceased to exist 1,200 years after its legendary foundation.

From 476 Italy was controlled by Germanic kings with their court at Ravenna. The first king was Odoacer, who had been elected by his German troops. The new rulers did much to sustain the Roman way of life and its traditions, and even restored some of the public monuments. In 489 Theoderic, King of the Ostrogoths in the Balkans, was asked to recover Italy for the Eastern Empire, but instead he defeated and killed Odoacer and had himself proclaimed king, ruling from 493 to 526.

THE RISE OF THE EAST

While the west was torn apart, the Eastern Empire, usually called the Byzantine Empire, remained largely unscathed and relatively free of invasion. Under the long and stable reign of Theodosius II (who replaced the emperor Arcadius in 408), the city of Constantinople continued to grow. Many churches were constructed in this 'Rome of the East', and a colossal system of defences was built after the West had fallen. The death of Theodosius II in 450 marked the end of the dynasty of Theodosius in the east, to be replaced by a succession of military emperors. Justinian

LES ANTIQUES

LEFT *The monumental arch at Glanum in southern France has survived exceptionally well as the site became virtually deserted.*

then ascended the throne in 527, and in the 38 years of his reign Constantinople was transformed and the Eastern Empire rose to a powerful position. In 532 serious riots in Constantinople caused large parts of the city to be burnt, and so a phase of imposing reconstruction and building was undertaken. The most important aspect of Justinian's reign, though, was the reorganization and codification of Roman law.

The previous emperor, Justin, had tried to encourage the estranged Churches of the west to move closer to those of the east. This policy was continued by his nephew Justinian, which caused much hostility. From 533, Justinian proceeded to win back the Western Empire, including Italy, Africa and parts of Spain. Starting in Africa, his general Belisarius extended the reconquest to Italy two years later. This campaign lasted until 554 and was accompanied by much destruction and violence.

Up to that point, senatorial life had continued at Rome, and Rome and Italy had continued to flourish under the Germanic kings. However, after the Byzantine recon-quest, the senatorial class disappeared, with many senators being forced to flee to Constantinople. As a result Ravenna became the seat of the new Byzantine government, while the rest of Italy, including Rome, was neglected and became impoverished. It is the demise and neglect of Rome that marks the end of the Classical world.

Justinian died in 565, but the Byzantine Empire survived for another 900 years until conquered by the Ottoman Turks in 1453. In 568 Italy was invaded by the Lombards, a west Germanic people previously settled in Pannonia (modern Hungary). Rome and Ravenna remained as Byzantine enclaves while the Lombards took over a large part of Italy, but Ravenna finally fell to the Lombards in 751 and slipped into obscurity. In the 7th and 8th centuries, much of the Eastern Empire, North Africa and parts of the Western Empire fell to invading Moors. In Constantinople, though, the walls of Theodosius II protected the city until 13 April, 1204 when armies of the Fourth Crusade broke through and devastated the magnificent city – in the name of Christianity.

SURVIVAL AND LEGACY

The survival of Roman buildings and structures such as aqueducts, of movable objects such as statues, sarcophagi and jewellery, varies across the Empire. Due to a scarcity of documentary and archaeological evidence, the history of this survival through the Middle Ages to the present day is often little known. This was not helped by those excavators who removed all medieval and later layers in order to reach was what underneath.

The Romans themselves destroyed much of their own work during the process of re-building over the centuries. Building stone and sculptures were frequently re-used; architectural fragments are often found built into city walls, and the relief sculptures on the Arch of Constantine in Rome, for example, were taken from a previous gateway or arch. On the other hand, the Romans also restored monuments which were of special significance to them.

During the 4th and 5th centuries, town and countryside were in a state of decline and abandonment in the Western Empire. Many public buildings had already fallen into decay and disuse before the Germanic invasions, although invasion did not necessarily mean wholesale destruction. In many towns, classical buildings continued to be used and repaired, but because of a decreasing population much of the countryside was de-populated, and towns shrank in size, or were even abandoned.

In the Middle Ages many people were surrounded by reminders of their Classical past, especially by buildings and structures. Even in the Saxon period there was an awareness

ABOVE Throughout history, stone from Hadrian's Wall was re-used as building stone. Evidence of the wall and the forts can be seen incorporated into many of the buildings and castles in the area.

OPPOSITE PAGE The Roman amphitheatre is still a symbol of entertainment at Nîmes, where the building is very well preserved allowing events to be staged – including bull fights, the modern-day equivalent of 'venationes'.

of the ancient civilization that had been lost, as is seen in the Anglo-Saxon poem *The Ruin* which probably describes the ruins of the Roman town of Bath. Much was still visible even up to the 18th century; it is only the present century which has destroyed Roman remains at an accelerating rate, often without record, and mainly by urban expansion and deep ploughing.

In places which were abandoned and well away from habitation, or where trading routes changed, whole Roman towns could be preserved, some in better condition than others, often depending on the climate. Les Antiques – a mausoleum and an archway – have survived virtually intact on the old Italy-to-Spain route at the town of Glanum (near St Rémy-de-Provence) in France. Other abandoned remains have decayed to such an extent that they are now mainly covered by fields, as is the case with the towns of Silchester and Wroxeter in England. Outside Europe, sculpture and architecture often survived virtually intact for centuries because population pressures tended to be much less.

Deserted sites were often used as quarries for building stone, which can then be identified in the buildings of the surrounding countryside. Some Roman towns were later reoccupied, but with a different street alignment, in ignorance of the previous grid plan. In those towns which continued to be occupied, buildings and monuments were robbed of their building materials with little regard for what was being destroyed. A number of Roman buildings do, however, survive intact, and at Arles in France the theatre and amphitheatre are still used today for performances. Some pagan games continued into the Christian era, and so amphitheatres tended to survive up to the 6th century. Theatres and amphitheatres were often incorporated into the defensive system of a town (as happened from the 8th century at Arles), and were later used as housing as well.

In the later Roman period, pagan temples were sometimes converted into churches, which assisted their preservation, as were other secular buildings such as baths. At Nîmes in France the Roman temple survives in exceptional condition; it is called the Maison Carrée, probably because of its use as the main city mosque (*cabah* or square house) in the 8th century when under Arab rule, but before then it served as a hall of justice.

Moison Corrée et Nesmel Nouvrrau

RIGHT The Maison Carrée temple at Nîmes survives virtually intact. It dates from the very beginning of the 1st century and was dedicated to the imperial cult. For a brief period it was converted to a mosque when the area was under Arab rule.

Some Roman towns became gradually hidden from view through decay, silting and the build-up of debris. This occurred at Rome which apparently became an unsavoury place in which to live. In many urban centres, the Roman deposits are a considerable depth below the modern-day street levels because of this build-up of debris.

In the countryside, many Roman roads continued to be used, as they are today, and Roman milestones and other monuments were retained as markers. That many Roman monuments were visible for centuries is witnessed in the many early documents relating to land where such monuments were mentioned as land markers.

Very large objects such as Trajan's Column in Rome also survived, but the fate of the enormous numbers of statues is not known except in very few cases. Many pagan statues were destroyed or defaced through religious intolerance or fear, while some were hidden and others left in place to decay. Bronze statues were melted down for their metal and marble ones were burnt in limekilns. Some statuary began to be collected during the Middle Ages, but more favoured were the sarcophagi, particularly decorated ones, which were re-used for Christian burials.

The written word has survived as inscriptions on dedications, tombstones and altars, and occasionally on parchment, papyrus and on writing tablets. Originally there must have been hundreds of thousands of manuscripts in the public and private libraries, but very few originals survive, even in fragments. Between 550 and 750 some manuscripts were copied, and the originals probably disintegrated or else the parchments were scraped clean for re-use. In the Middle Ages, however, more and more of the surviving manuscripts were copied in monasteries, ensuring the preservation of some texts today.

Throughout the Roman period, the native people gradually learned to speak and write fluent Latin, leading to the disappearance of many other languages and dialects. In the Eastern Empire Greek continued to be the main language, although the language itself underwent a continuous process of modification. In the west, the pronunciation of Latin varied regionally, but in Britain Latin died away with the Germanic invasions towards the end of the Roman period. Instead, English developed, only to be influenced by Latin and Greek during the conversion of the country to Christianity from the 6th century. Elsewhere in the Western Empire the Church helped to retain Latin and, until the end of the Medieval period, the language remained the main medium of communication of all well-educated people. By 700 everyday Latin was evolving into what are now called the Romance languages (French, Italian, Romanian, and others).

During the Renaissance classical Latin, by

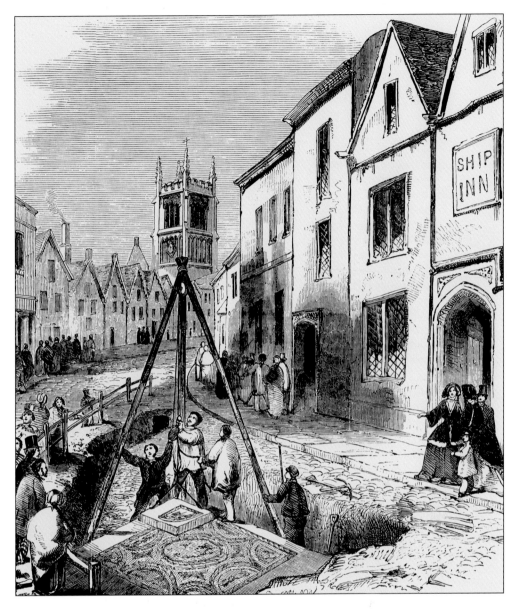

RIGHT The modern-day level of many towns is considerably higher than that of the Roman remains. A mid 19th-century discovery of a mosaic at Cirencester in England was well below the level of the street.

BELOW RIGHT The amphitheatre at Arles is a popular tourist attraction. It was transformed into a fortified stronghold in the Medieval period. As well as a fort, it was also used for housing, but in 1825 the amphitheatre was cleared of all the houses and was excavated. The tower was part of the medieval fort.

then a dead language, experienced a rival. There was an awakening of interest in Classical studies, which has continued to the present day. The study of Roman architecture and art greatly influenced architectural and art styles in Europe from the Renaissance onwards. Interest in all things Roman continues to grow even though the Classics, including Latin, are rarely taught in schools. Much more than that, the Romans have affected our everyday lives, in areas such as jurisdiction, town planning, art, coinage design and even our language. It is an unfortunate irony that while there is an increasing interest in the Romans, and modern research methods add to our knowledge about them, more and more of their remains are being destroyed with little or no record.

GLOSSARY

amphitheatre: an oval arena surrounded by seats for mass entertainment.

amphorae: very large pottery vessels for transporting products such as wine, olive oil and fish sauce.

aqueduct: a system of conducting water in pipes, channels in the ground, or channels supported on arches.

Augusti: co-emperors of the Eastern and Western Empires.

auxiliaries: soldiers recruited from non-Roman citizens.

Barbarians: a Greek term adopted by the Romans to describe foreigners or non-Romans.

basilica: aisled building often associated with the forum.

Byzantine Empire: the Eastern Roman Empire from the time of Constantine I until 1453.

Caesars: co-rulers of the eastern and western empires, below the rank of Augusti.

camp: a temporary fortified enclosure with tents for housing military troops.

Carthaginians: a powerful sea-faring nation in North Africa, who were originally Phoenicians from the Lebanon.

Celtic: a term used to describe people who inhabited northern Europe in the Iron Age.

centuriation: a system of dividing the land into regular blocks.

cohort: a unit of auxiliaries or legionaries.

colonies: deliberate foundations of towns, usually settled by veteran soldiers.

contubernium: tent-party of 8 soldiers.

Etruscans: a tribe controlling much of central and northern Italy from the 8th century BC and who established many cities.

fortresses: permanent establishments for legionary troops.

forts: permanent establishments for auxiliary troops.

forum: civic centre, usually a square surrounded by offices, a temple and a basilica.

Gaul: modern-day France and Germany west of the Rhine; inhabited by Celtic peoples usually referred to as Gauls.

hypocaust: underfloor heating system.

Iron Age: a period of prehistory when iron was used as the main technological material.

latifundia: large agricultural estates.

Latin: language of the Romans. Also used to describe the people from the tribes south of Rome in the district of Latium.

legionaries: soldiers recruited from Roman citizens.

Livy: Roman historian, 59 BC–AD 17.

mausolea: stone-built structures for housing the dead, usually in coffins.

mosaic: a patterned floor or wall made from thousands of tiny cubes (usually of stone).

odeum: a small, permanently roofed theatre for musical performances and recitations.

patricians: aristocratic members of society.

Phoenicians: *see* Carthaginians.

plebeians: the urban poor.

Praetorian Guard: personal bodyguard and élite force of the emperor.

Punic Wars: fought against the Phoenicians, called *Poeni* by the Romans, which in turn gave the English term 'Punic'.

quernstones: stones for grinding grain into flour.

Romanization: the gradual adoption of the Roman way of life by non-Romans.

Sabines: a tribe to the north of Rome.

Samnites: a tribe to the south of Rome.

sarcophagi: stone coffins.

Senate: ruling council at Rome.

Tetrarchy: four-man rule of the empire.

veterans: retired soldiers.

villa: a country house, often with mosaics and wall paintings, and normally part of an agricultural estate.

votive offering: an offering or gift to a god.

wooden writing tablets: flat pieces of wood, with a layer of wax. Writing was done with a metal implement (*stylus*) on the wax, and could be erased by being heated and smoothed over. The writing sometimes scored the wood beneath, so preserving the messages.

SOME BOOKS TO READ

BOARDMAN, J., J. GRIFFIN and O. MURRAY (eds). 1988. *The Roman World* (Oxford University Press, Oxford and New York). Illustrated descriptions of the history and social life of Classical Rome, with particular emphasis on the contemporary literature.

CHEVALLIER, R. 1976. *Roman Roads* (Batsford, London). Gives much information on Roman roads, including methods of construction, bridges, life on the roads, and evidence from literature and inscriptions.

CLAYTON, P. *The Treasures of Ancient Rome* (Bison Books, London). 1986. Records Rome's artistic achievement and also an informative account of the Roman Empire as seen through its visible remains, artefacts and monuments. Heavily illustrated.

CONNOLLY, P. 1981. *Greece and Rome at War* (Macdonald, London). Vividly illustrated account of classical warfare, including numerous colour drawings and reconstructions.

CORNELL, T., and J. MATTHEWS, 1982. *Atlas of the Roman World* (Phaidon, Oxford). Charts the development of Rome and its Empire from the earliest times to the Byzantine Empire, copiously illustrated with maps, plans, photographs, and diagrams.

GREENE, K. 1986. *The Archaeology of the Roman Economy* (Batsford, London). A useful book on the economy throughout the Empire, including transport, coinage, agriculture, and industry.

GREENHALGH, M. 1989. *The Survival of Roman Antiquities in the Middle Ages* (Duckworth, London). Describes the survival into the Middle Ages of buildings and other structures, as well as smaller objects and manuscripts, from the Western Roman Empire.

HARDEN, D.B. 1987. *Glass of the Caesars* (Olivetti, Milan). Explains the wide-ranging techniques of Roman glass manufacturers, with numerous examples illustrated in colour; essentially an exhibition catalogue.

HENIG, M. 1984. *Religion in Roman Britain* (Batsford, London). Illustrated account of the many aspects of Roman religion, with evidence drawn largely from Britain.

JACKSON, R. 1988. *Doctors and Diseases in the Roman Empire* (British Museum Publications, London). Fascinating illustrated book on many aspects of Roman medicine and hygiene, from birth-control to death.

JOHNSON, A. 1983. *Roman Forts of the 1st and 2nd centuries AD in Britain and the German Provinces* (A. & C. Black, London). Well-illustrated account of various aspects of Roman forts.

JOHNSON, S. 1989. *Hadrian's Wall* (Batsford, London). History and everyday life of one of the Empire's frontiers; numerous illustrations.

PERCIVAL, J. 1976. *The Roman Villa, An Historical Introduction* (Batsford, London). Includes many details on Roman villas across the Empire.

SHELTON, J-A. 1988. *As The Romans Did. A Sourcebook in Roman Social History* (Oxford University Press, Oxford and New York). Discusses various aspects of social life, with examples in English translation from contemporary texts and inscriptions.

STRONG, D., and D. BROWN, (eds). 1976. *Roman Crafts* (Duckworth, London). An illustrated guide to the arts and crafts of the Romans.

WACHER, J. 1974. *The Towns of Roman Britain* (Batsford, London). How towns developed and what they were like in one Roman province.

EVENTS IN THE ROMAN WORLD AND ELSEWHERE

ROMAN HISTORY		EVENTS ELSEWHERE	
753 BC	Foundation of Rome	671 BC	Assyrian conquest of Egypt
		612 BC	Nimrud destroyed
		c. 600 BC	Greek colony founded at Marseille
509 BC	Foundation of the Republic	480 BC	Athens sacked by Persians
		479 BC	Death of Confucius
		432 BC	Completion of the Parthenon at Athens
390 BC	Rome sacked by Gauls	350 BC	Crossbow invented in China
		323 BC	Death of Alexander the Great
275 BC	Roman victory over King Pyrrhus of Epirus		
264–241 BC	First Punic War	221 BC	Great Wall of China built
218–201 BC	Second Punic War		
216 BC	Romans defeated at Battle of Cannae	206 BC	Chang'an becomes capital of Han dynasty in China
149–146 BC	Third Punic War		
146 BC	Corinth destroyed by Romans		
133 BC	Tiberius Gracchus' land reforms	c. 112 BC	Opening of Silk Road from China to West
81 BC	Sulla becomes dictator		
60 BC	Formation of First Triumvirate		
49 BC	Julius Caesar invades Italy		
44 BC	Julius Caesar is assassinated		
31 BC	Octavian defeats Antony at Actium	31 BC	Stela of this date from the Olmec site of Tres Zapotes, Mexico
AD c. 30	Crucifixion of Jesus		
43	Invasion of Britain by Claudius	c. 50	Teotihuacán in Mexico laid out as a city
64	Great Fire at Rome		
70	Destruction of Jerusalem by Titus		
79	Eruption of Vesuvius	105	First use of paper in China
166	Plague sweeps Empire		
212	Citizenship conferred throughout Empire	271	Magnetic compass in use in China
		300	Classic period of Maya civilization begins
313	Edict of Milan		
378	Romans defeated at Adrianpole		
401	Milan besieged by Visigoths		
410	Rome captured and sacked by Visigoths	c. 450	Germanic villages abandoned due to flooding
451	Attila the Hun defeated		
455	Rome sacked by Vandals		
476	Last of the western Roman emperors deposed	c. 550	Buddhism introduced into Japan
533–554	Reconquest of the western Empire		
568	Italy invaded by the Lombards	600	Mesa Verde occupied in USA

EMPERORS OF THE ROMAN WORLD

27 BC–AD 14	Augustus
14–37	Tiberius
37–41	Gaius (Caligula)
41–54	Claudius
54–68	Nero
68–69	Galba
69	Otho
69	Vitellius
67–79	Vespasian
79–81	Titus
81–96	Domitian
96–98	Nerva
98–117	Trajan
117–138	Hadrian
138–161	Antoninus Pius
161–180	Marcus Aurelius
161–169	Lucius Verus
180–193	Commodus
193	Pertinax
193	Didius Julianus
193–211	Septimius Severus
211–212	Geta
211–217	Caracalla
217–218	Macrinus
218–222	Elagabalus
222–235	Alexander Severus
235–238	Maximinus
238	Gordian I
238	Gordian II
238	Balbinus
238	Pupienus
238–244	Gordian III
244–249	Philip the Arab
249–251	Decius
251–253	Trebonianus Gallus
2511–253	Volusianus
253	Aemilianus
253–260	Valerian
253–268	Gallienus
268–270	Claudius II, Gothicus
270	Quintillus
270–275	Aurelian
275–276	Tacitus
276	Florian
276–282	Probus
282–283	Carus
283–284	Carinus
283–284	Numerianus
284–305	Diocletian

EMPERORS OF THE ROMAN WORLD

WEST		EAST	
286–305	Maximain (Augustus)	286–305	Dioletian (Augustus)
293–305	Constantanius Chlorus (Caesar)	293–305	Galerius (Caesar)
305–306	Constantius Chlorus (Augustus)	305–311	Galerius (Augustus)
305	Severus (Caesar)	305–309	Maximinus (Caesar)
306–307	Severus (Augustus)	309–313	Maximinus (Augustus)
306–312	Maxentius (Augustus)		
306–307	Constantine (Caesar)	308–324	Licinius (Augustus)
307–324	Constantine (Augustus)		
324–337 Constantine I			
317–337	Constantine II (Caesar)	317	Licinianus (Caesar)
337–340	Constantine II (Augustus)	317–326	Crispus (Caesar)
333–337	Constans (Caesar)	324–337	Constantius II (Caesar)
337–350	Constans (Augustus)	337–361	Constantius II (Augustus)
350–353	Magnentius (usurper, Augustus)	335–337	Dalmatius (Caesar)
353–361 Constantius II			
355–361	Julian (Caesar)	350–354	Gallus (Caesar)
361–363 Julian			
363–364 Jovian			
364–375	Valentinian I	364–378	Valens
375–383	Gratian	379–395	Theodosius I
375–392	Valentinian II		
383–388	Magnus Maximus (usurper)		
392–394	Eugenius (usurper)		
392–395 Theodosius I			
395–423	Honorius	395–408	Arcadius
423–425	Iohannes (usurper)	408–450	Theodosius II
425–455	Valentinian III	450–457	Marcian
455	Petronius Maximus		
455–456	Avitus		
457–461	Majorian	457–474	Leo
461–465	Libius Severus		
467–472	Anthemius		
472	Olybrius		
473	Glycerius		
473–475	Nepos	474–491	Zeno
475–476	Romulus Augustulus	475–476	Basiliscus

BARBARIAN KINGS OF ITALY

WEST		EAST	
476–493	Odoacer	491–518	Anastasius
493–526	Theoderic	518–527	Justin
526–534	Athalaric	527–565	Justinian
534–536	Theodahad		

INDEX

Page numbers in italics refer to captions and pictures.

PICTURE CREDITS

LESLEY AND ROY ADKINS – pp 7, 19, 22, 24, 28 top, 38, 44, 45 top and bottom, 47, 52–54 top and bottom, 57 bottom left and right, 61 top, 65 bottom, 67, 70, 74, 82 top and bottom, 83, 87 top, 91, 96–7, 100 left, 107 bottom, 111 bottom, 115, 116–7, 120, 121 bottom

C M DIXON – pp 6, 9 top, 11–15, 20, 21, 23, 25 bottom, 26 top, 29, 34–5, 37, 51, 55, 57 top, 58–9, 61 bottom, 62–3, 65 top, 66 top and bottom, 68 top, 69, 72–3, 75, 78, 85, 86, 88 top, 89, 94, 95 bottom, 99, 100 right, 101, 102, 103 top, 104, 105 bottom, 106, 109 top

MUSEUM OF LONDON – pp 25 top, 26 bottom, 28 bottom, 31 top, 39, 42–3, 49, 60, 68 bottom,

77, 80–1, 84, 87 top, 88 bottom, 95 top, 103 bottom, 107 top, 109 bottom, 111 top, 113

MICK SHARP – pp 16–7, 31 bottom, 33, 36, 92

NATIONAL GALLERIES OF SCOTLAND – pp 118

THE ILLUSTRATED LONDON NEWS PICTURE LIBRARY – pp 48, 121

BRITISH MUSEUM – pp 114

BODLEIAN LIBRARY OXFORD – pp 110

DAVE LONGLEY – pp 105 top

MUSEUM OF ANTIQUITIES NEWCASTLE-UPON-TYNE – pp 40, 41

MISS R J WILSON – pp 30, 50

A GILBERT – pp 9 bottom